Weekends for Two in Northern California

Second Edition

Weekends for Two in

Northern California

50

ROMANTIC GETAWAYS

Revised and Updated
Second Edition

BILL GLEESON
PHOTOGRAPHS BY
JOHN SWAIN

CONTENTS

ACKNOWLEDGMENTS

The author and photographer wish to thank the following people for their contributions, inspiration, and support.

Krista Hendricks, Editorial and Research Assistance
Regina Miesch, Photographic Styling
Yvonne Gleeson, Research Assistance
Jerry Hulse

Second Edition
Printed in Hong Kong.

Library of Congress Cataloging-in-Publication Data:

Gleeson, Bill.
    Weekends for two in Northern California : 50 romantic getaways / Bill Gleeson ; photographs by John Swain.
        p.   cm.
"Completely revised and updated"—Cover
    Includes index.
    ISBN 0-8118-0536-0
    1. Hotels—California, Northern—Guidebooks.
2. California, Northern—Guidebooks. I. Title.
TX907.3.C2G54 1994   93-40081
647.9479401—dc20   CIP

Distributed in Canada by Raincoast Books,
8680 Cambie Street, Vancouver, B.C. V6P 6M9

10 9 8 7 6 5 4 3 2

Chronicle Books
85 Second Street
San Francisco, CA 94105

INTRODUCTION

Dual careers, sixty-hour work weeks, soccer, and softball.... Chances are it's been awhile since you stole away together—just the two of you. For us, at least, the time between getaways is usually measured in months, even seasons.

Given their special nature (and infrequency), weekend trips for two are nothing to take lightly. We approach such occasions with a strategy that most would reserve for a round-the-world tour: maps, brochures, guidebooks, restaurant reviews, and itineraries, not to mention overnight babysitters and back-up overnight babysitters.

After a particularly long stretch of nursing sick children, home-improvement projects,
bad weather, and other commitments, the two of us decided to flee to the coast for two days of togetherness. After thumbing through our bed-and-breakfast guides and a handful of dog-eared hotel brochures, we settled on a quaint, romantic inn and phoned in a reservation.

A few days later we received in the mail our confirmation along with a colorful booklet with stunning color photos of a suite with canopied bed, a bathroom with fireplace, and an oval tub-for-two. It wasn't until we checked in that we learned there was only one such suite. Since it was already taken, we settled for a small room with a squeaky mattress. All we could do was shoot dirty looks at the smiling, contented couple emerging from the room with the bathroom fireplace.

Most of us can probably recall a similar experience—being referred by friends to a quiet, romantic inn or hotel, only to be assigned a room in one of three categories: those directly over the restaurant kitchen, the ones next to an elevator shaft, or the rooms overlooking a noisy or neon-lit street.

This book is intended to help minimize the element of chance that can cloud a cherished weekend for two and to help ensure that this special time away together lives up to your expectations.

Rooms for Romance

When we set about documenting Northern California's most romantic destinations, we looked for a variety of special features. Our romantic criteria included:
- Private bathrooms
- In-room fireplaces
- Tubs or showers big enough for two
- Breakfast in bed or in your room
- Feather beds and cushy comforters
- Canopied, four-poster, king-sized beds
- Private decks, patios, or balconies with inspirational views
- Romantic decor, special touches, and accessories

We also sought out hotels and inns that exude that overall, sometimes difficult-to-describe intimate atmosphere and those that discourage child guests, since many couples are seeking a well-deserved break from the kids.

Within the inns and small hotels listed in this book, we discovered special rooms that are particularly conducive to a romantic experience. Instead of leaving the choice of rooms to the reservation clerk and describing in detail the public areas of each establishment, we've devoted a good part of this book to details of particularly romantic rooms and suites. When booking your getaway reservation, don't hesitate to ask about the availability of a specific room—unless, of course, you already have a personal favorite.

We've also identified particularly noteworthy restaurants in a few locations. However, these change often. The fact is, the inns listed here enjoy providing visitors with information about restaurants and other diversions that will enhance that special occasion.

Cast Your Vote

Speaking of favorite getaway destinations, we'd like to know about yours. We invite you to use the form at the back of this book to cast your vote for Northern California's most romantic destination. And if we overlooked one of your special places, please write to us in care of Chronicle Books, 275 Fifth Street, San Francisco, CA 94103. We look forward to sharing new romantic weekends for two in future printings.

A Word About Rates

While seasoned travelers might still be able to find a room along California's well-traveled highways for less than $50, this guide isn't for bargain hunters. Since romantic getaways are special occasions, we've learned to adjust to the higher tariffs being commanded for a special room. In fact, most of the rooms described in the following pages start at more than $100 per night.

To help you plan your getaway budget, approximate 1994 rates for specific rooms are noted within and at the end of each description. If you're booking a weekend trip, please note that some of the more popular establishments require two-night minimum stays.

Rates (in 1994; per weekend night for two friendly people) are classified at the end of each listing in the following ranges, not including tax:

Moderate: Under $150
Expensive: $150-$200
Deluxe: Over $200

Final Notes

No payment was sought or accepted from any establishment in exchange for a listing in this book.

Food, wine, and flowers were often added to photos for styling purposes. Some inns provide such amenities; others do not. Please ask when making a reservation whether these items are complimentary or whether they're provided for an extra charge.

The author cannot guarantee that these properties will maintain furnishings or standards as they existed on our visit, and we very much appreciate hearing from readers if their experience is at variance with our descriptions. Reader comments were carefully consulted in the creation of this revised edition. Your opinions are important.

THE NORTH COAST

Daytime Diversions

If your legs are up to it, hike down the more than four-hundred steps to the Point Reyes Lighthouse at the National Seashore. It's a great place to snuggle against the wind and watch passing whales some three hundred feet below.

Twelve miles north of Jenner, and definitely worth a visit, is Fort Ross State Historic Park, a reconstructed fortress established by Russian seal hunters in the early 1800s.

In Mendocino, rent a canoe at Stanford Inn by the Sea. (See separate entry for a description of the inn.) Innkeeper Jeff Stanford has set up Catch a Canoe, a boat rental service under the bridge at the mouth of Big River just south of the village. Big River flows through a narrow, undeveloped redwood canyon. You can rent by the hour or overnight. Bicycles are also available.

Farther north, near Garberville, leave Highway 101 for a scenic, thirty-three-mile detour through the old redwoods along Avenue of the Giants.

Tables for Two

The Olema Inn and Manka's in Inverness are good choices for travelers staying in the Point Reyes area. St. Orres, the beautiful Russian-style inn located in Gualala, has a well-respected dining room that serves fixed-price dinners. If you find yourself near the Benbow Inn (near Garberville) around dinner, try the inn's highly rated restaurant. In Eureka, consistently memorable meals are served in the dining room at The Carter House.

In Mendocino, we recommend 955 Ukiah and Cafe Beaujolais, also on Ukiah Street. These are within walking distance of our Mendocino destinations. In Little River, try the Little River Restaurant.

After Hours

Our advice: Retreat to your inn and cozy up to a warm fire.

Point Reyes Seashore Lodge

10021 Coastal Highway 1
P.O. Box 39, Olema, CA 94950
Telephone: (415) 663-9000

Eighteen rooms and three suites, each with private bath. Suites include wet bars/refrigerators, featherbeds, whirlpool tubs, coffeemakers, and morning newspaper. Continental breakfast. Smoking is discouraged. Handicapped access. Moderate to Expensive.

Getting There
The inn is two miles south of the community of Point Reyes on Highway 1, a one-hour drive from San Francisco, two-and-a-half hours from Sacramento.

POINT REYES SEASHORE LODGE

Olema

*M*ost any weekend, when Tahoe- and beach-bound traffic has highways leading out of the Bay Area tied in knots, the smart money is cruising north. Driving through the lush pastures and hills of west Marin County, you'll probably encounter more cows than cars.

While funky, old burgs like Bolinas, Point Reyes, and Olema have attracted a steady but slow flow of visitors over the years, there's a new reason (besides the whales) to venture up here. It may have been built a century after many of the historic inns that dot the countryside, but the Point Reyes Seashore Lodge was fashioned in a grand, graceful style that fits right in with its Victorian neighbors.

Tom and Jeff Harriman built the inn in 1988 with a goal toward providing just the right touches for intimate encounters. They started with a choice locale: a hillside spot that commands a view of a meadow and pine forest. Hidden by the inn from the parking areas, the panorama is especially entrancing when it unfolds for the first time to visitors entering their rooms.

Guest rooms here are compact, but the generous use of glass makes them appear much larger. Rooms along the upper floor have either bay windows or porches, while some lower-level rooms have decks.

Rooms for Romance

It is impossible to go wrong with any of the nine top-floor rooms. However, some are particularly well-suited to romance. Room 18, the Sir Francis Drake Suite, is a split-level affair with a step-down living space equipped with fireplace and refrigerator. A spectacular clerestory bay window rises from floor to ceiling and provides a view even from the paneled sleeping loft.

Placement of the spa tub allows bathers an unusual opportunity to look out under the stairs through the window to the treetops beyond. There's room for two in the tub in a pinch.

Next door, the mauve-toned Garcia Rancho Suite (Room 19) is a close second, with sleeping loft, spa tub, fireplace, and French doors that open to a tiny deck. The Audubon Suite (Room 17) is similarly styled.

For convivial guests, continental breakfast can be taken in the downstairs dining room in front of a rock-walled fireplace. Those seeking more privacy may load their trays with pastries, juice, fruit, and cereal and retreat to their rooms.

In all, the lodge offers only twenty-one rooms and suites, and weekend reservations for the best suites should be made a few weeks in advance.

By the way, before setting off for weather-fickle Olema, be sure to bring clothing for both sun and fog, regardless of season. That is unless you don't plan to leave your room. In that case, only the bare essentials are required.

Seacliff

39140 South Highway 1
(P.O. Box 697), Gualala, CA 95445
Telephone: (707) 884-1213

Sixteen rooms, each with private bath, spa tub, fireplace, deck, and refrigerator. No in-room phones.
Amenities include chilled champagne, bubblebath,
and binoculars. Non-smoking rooms available.
Handicapped access. Moderate to expensive.

Getting There
From the Bay Area, take Highway 101 past Santa
Rosa to River Road. West to Highway 116 and west
to Jenner. Head north on Highway 1 to Gualala.
Driving time from San Francisco is two and a half
hours.

SEACLIFF

Gualala

$\mathcal{E}$ven with music playing softly, we could hear the not-so-distant nighttime surf pound the Gualala beach. Add a flickering fire and you've got the fixings for a sensual feast that's well worth the two-and-a-half-hour drive from the Bay Area.

The inn's sixteen rooms are spread among clusters of four that perch on a steep bluff overlooking the Pacific Ocean and Gualala River. (The river separates the inn from the beach, so the seashore, although very close, isn't immediately accessible on foot.)

Rooms for Romance

Seacliff's rooms are compact but generously equipped. Each has a king-sized bed facing a fireplace and small, private deck. In the bathroom, a spa tub for two sits beneath an ocean-view window. The in-room refrigerator holds a complimentary bottle of champagne. Bubblebath provides the icing on the cake.

Although all rooms feature whitewater views and similar amenities, we suggest the upper-level accommodations for a bit more privacy and slightly elevated river and ocean vista. The second-floor rooms also feature cathedral ceilings. All are offered in the mid to upper $100 range.

WHALE WATCH INN

35100 Highway 1
Gualala, CA 95445
Telephone: (707) 884-3667

Eighteen rooms and suites, each with private bath, fireplace, deck, bubblebath, and ice maker; eight with whirlpool tubs for two. Five units have complete kitchens. Breakfast with hot entree delivered to your room (included in price). Two-night minimum stay on weekends; three-night minimum on holiday weekends. Smoking permitted on decks only. Handicapped access. Expensive to deluxe.

Getting There
From the Bay Area, take Highway 101 past Santa Rosa to River Road. West to Highway 116 and west to Jenner. Head north on Highway 1 to Gualala. Driving time from San Francisco is two and a half hours. Inn is five miles north of Gualala.

WHALE WATCH INN

Gualala

*U*nlike many north-coast inns, in which doilies and antiques prevail, the Whale Watch Inn dares to be different. With its pastel hues, interesting angles, and skylights, the inn offers a fresh touch of contemporary elegance and some of this region's most intimate rooms and soul-stirring views.

Occupying an unusual sunny, banana-belt spot of the coast, Whale Watch Inn is spread among five separate buildings on two wooded acres. A private stairway leads to a half-mile-long beach with tidal pools and sea lions. It's the stuff of which honeymoons are made. However, instead of the typical single bridal suite, each of Whale Watch Inn's eighteen rooms is honeymoon quality.

Rooms for Romance

First, the basics. Each room has an ocean view and a fireplace, as well as a private deck. But that's where the similarities stop. Every room has its own design, flow, and atmosphere. The following are a few of our favorites.

The Bath Suite is aptly named. While the sitting/sleeping area is impressive, wait until you ascend the spiral staircase. The dual spa tub under a skylight and Pacific view make this suite one of the inn's most popular. If you're planning a weekend visit, you'd be wise to make your reservation six months in advance. This room is offered in the mid $200 range.

Crystal Sea, a similarly priced second-floor room in the Quest building, offers a coastal view that, in our opinion, is unsurpassed in Northern California. While the ocean vista

alone would have sufficed, guests are treated to a moon and star view, compliments of a skylight over the bed. For dessert, there's a fireplace and a two-person whirlpool bath.

Silver Mist, a split-level suite done in soft silver gray and lavender, has an elevated dual spa tub that overlooks the fireplace, bed, and ocean beyond.

While the above three rooms carry nightly rates in the mid $200 range (two-night minimum on weekends), Whale Watch Inn does offer accommodations that go a bit easier on the budget. The cozy Rose Room, for example, features a four-poster, queen-sized bed, fireplace, and ocean-view deck for about $65 less.

Coast Guard House - Inn at Arena Cove

695 Arena Cove
Point Arena, CA 95468
Toll-free telephone: (800) 524-9320

Seven rooms, five with private baths; one with
whirlpool tub for two. Spa on site. Continental
vegetarian breakfast is served at a communal table.
Two-night minimum stay on some holiday weekends. Smoking permitted outside only. No handicapped access. Moderate to expensive.

Getting There
From Highway 101 at Petaluma, follow Highway
116 west to Bodega Bay. At Highway 1, drive north
past Jenner and Gualala to Point Arena. Turn left on
Iverson Avenue; inn is on the right.

COAST GUARD HOUSE - INN AT ARENA COVE

Point Arena

*N*ot so long ago, visitors seeking romance in Point Arena had to be content snuggling in a motel along Highway 1 or in a chilly beachside tent. Then, in 1989, along came Merita Whatley and Richey Wasserman who made this little community a full-fledged romantic destination by restoring a historic Cape Cod-style house overlooking the ocean.

Built by the Lifesaving Service at the turn of the century, the house once served the U.S. Coast Guard and stored lifeboats used to rescue shipwreck survivors. The nautical accents and antique furnishings sprinkled throughout the inn reflect the innkeepers' desire to keep the seaport lore alive.

A colorful garden grows edible flowers used to garnish the hearty vegetarian breakfasts served on anchorware dishes used on Navy and Coast Guard ships.

Outside, the resident pets lead guests to an ocean-view spa, where on one of those memorable, north coast starlit nights, the sound of the lapping surf lulls guests into another world.

Rooms for Romance

Just past the garden, secluded from the main house is a private cabin (high $100 range) which was being refurbished during our visit. Equipped with a spa tub for two and a fireplace, the cabin provides an unobstructed view of the Pacific.

In the main house, the Flag Room (low $100 range) boasts a queen-sized captain's bed nestled against three cove-side windows. Whitewashed walls, hardwood floors, and nautical antiques lend a Navy flavor, while fresh flowers, a fluffy down comforter, and a cozy tub for two in the adjoining sunken private bath soften the decor. A sunny nook with a window seat and brass foot rail overlooks the ocean.

Upstairs, Surfmen Cove (mid $100 range) graces the west side of the house, offering an ocean view, antique woodburning fireplace, and a Japanese-style tub for two in a private bath.

The Keepers Canyon and Cypress rooms share a bathroom.

Harbor House

5600 South Highway 1
(P.O. Box 369), Elk, CA 95432
Telephone: (707) 877-3203

Six rooms in main house and four cottage rooms.
Nine have fireplaces; all have private baths. Tariff
includes breakfast and dinner for two. Smoking is not
permitted. No handicapped access. Expensive to
deluxe.

Getting There

From the Bay Area, take Highway 101 to Cloverdale;
west on Highway 128 to Highway 1; south six miles
to inn. Elk is approximately three hours' driving time
from the Golden Gate Bridge.

Harbor House

*I*mpressive is what the Goodyear Redwood Lumber Company had in mind when it built this 1916 house as an executive residence and exclusive retreat for VIP guests. Although its architectural style might best be described as craftsman or bungalow, a simple bungalow it isn't.

Wandering through the front door we found ourselves in a fabulous parlor lounge crafted entirely of redwood, with vaulted ceiling, hand-rubbed (with beeswax as a preservative) paneling, and imposing fireplace. The entire inn is made of redwood, fashioned after an exhibit at the Panama-Pacific International Exposition in San Francisco.

Rooms for Romance

With a parlor as grand as the one that greets visitors here, it's possible our expectations were on the high side when we toured the guest rooms. While not as inspiring as the public area, the rooms were spacious and comfortable. And the ocean views rated four stars.

Rooms situated in the main house of many inns leave guests feeling like they're swimming in a goldfish bowl, but the six rooms under the Harbor House roof seemed quiet and private. Several rooms have been recarpeted since our first visit.

Among our favorite accommodations was Harbor, situated in a sunny corner on the second floor. A large room, it holds two queen-sized beds and antique furniture that included an English library table. This room also features a fireplace, old-style bathroom with shower, and a dramatic ocean view.

Beneath Harbor on the first floor was Cypress, a large room (low $200 range) with two king-sized beds, velvet lounger, fireplace, and a six-foot-long clawfoot soaking tub.

Four quaint, red-and-white cottage rooms, each with a fireplace, complete the Harbor House estate. Seaview holds a queen-sized bed and fireplace and is decorated with floral wallpaper and pine-paneled ceiling. Both Seaview and Oceansong offer sweeping ocean views. The Shorepine Cottage (offered in the mid $100 range) has a king-sized bed and a private deck with a view of both the woods and ocean.

After they've savored the sea from a cottage deck or from a guest-room window, guests usually head for the rear garden and the winding path that leads down to the water's edge. Along the way are sitting areas for sunning and schmoozing.

The inn's ocean-view dining room is the primary center of activity, as guests are treated not only to breakfast but dinner. (Lodging is on the modified American Plan.) Don't worry about having to make small talk with strangers, either; the proprietors thoughtfully set the room with tables for two.

Greenwood Pier Inn

5928 South Highway 1
(P.O. Box 36), Elk, CA 95432
Telephone: (707) 877-9997

Eleven rooms, each with private bath, fireplace, and
ocean-view deck. The cafe here serves dinners to
guests and passersby Friday and Saturday nights. On
the other nights, inn guests can have dinner delivered
to their rooms. Continental breakfast delivered to
your room. Minimum two-night stay on weekends
and during holidays. No restrictions on smoking.
Handicapped access. Moderate to expensive.

Getting There
From the Bay Area, take Highway 101 to Cloverdale,
west on Highway 128 to Highway 1; south six miles
to inn. Greenwood Pier Inn is five miles south of
Highway 128 turnoff on Highway 1. Elk is approximately three hours' driving time from the Golden
Gate Bridge.

GREENWOOD PIER INN

Situated between Highway 1 and the sea, the Greenwood Pier Inn was recommended by some folks who raved about its new SeaCastle building overlooking the Pacific. Expecting to find a contemporary establishment, we were surprised to discover a venerable, eclectic collection of still-evolving accommodations, of which SeaCastle represents only the latest chapter.

Innkeepers Kendrick and Isabel Petty have been Elk residents for more than two decades, and their influence is felt throughout the inn. Isabel, in addition to being a talented baker, created the adjacent country store as well as the quilt art that graces the guest rooms. In addition to serving as the inn's resident chef, Kendrick cultivated the colorful grounds and is responsible for the tile and marble work in many of the rooms.

Rooms for Romance

For purposes of this book, we've limited our recommendations to three accommodations. The two guest rooms in SeaCastle (mid to upper $100 range) are as romantic as you'll find

along this part of the north coast. Constructed in an unusual Roman/Victorian style, SeaCastle is perched at the edge of a cliff overlooking the ocean and beautiful rock formations. A sitting room occupies the lower floor, just below the sleeping quarters. A spiral staircase leads to the bathroom loft, which features an ocean view and marble tub for two. Both SeaCastle rooms have fireplaces.

If SeaCastle is booked, you might consider Cliffhouse, a large, rustic ocean-view cabin sitting on the edge of a cliff. Cliffhouse (mid $100 range) is paneled in redwood and features a marble fireplace and spa tub for two. There's also a private, ocean-view deck at cliff's edge with lounges and chairs—for the not so faint of heart.

Albion River Inn

3790 North Highway 1
(P.O. Box 100), Albion, CA 95410
Telephone: (707) 937-1919

Twenty rooms, each with private bath; sixteen with
fireplaces; ten with oversized or spa tubs; fourteen
with private decks. Amenities include wine and
chocolates in guest rooms. Breakfast (served in dining
room) included. Restaurant and bar. Two-night minimum stay during weekends; three-night minimum
stay during some holiday periods. Smoking is not permitted. Handicapped access. Moderate to deluxe.

Getting There

Albion is six miles south of Mendocino. From San
Francisco, take Highway 101 north past Cloverdale.
Head west on Highway 128 to Highway 1. North
two miles to inn. Driving time from San Francisco is
approximately three and a half hours.

ALBION RIVER INN

*W*ho says cottages by the sea have to be old and rustic? Since many we've been introduced to seem to fit that description, we were surprised to discover Albion River Inn, a newer cluster of cozy, freestanding cottages (mixed with attractive multiroom units) designed specifically with vacationing romantics in mind.

The inn's architecture is East Coast-inspired, but its setting is pure California coast. The Albion River empties into the ocean here; each of the inn's twenty rooms affords views of this picturesque meeting of river and sea. Forested hills to the east provide the backdrop.

Rooms for Romance

Room 1 has a pitched roof and is equipped with a tiled fireplace that separates the king-sized bed from the bathroom. Room 5, a freestanding cottage, is similarly styled, but also has a small, private deck. Both contain spa tubs for two.

Willow furnishings and mature, potted plants give Room 4 an unconventional look. The pitched-ceilinged room is paneled in light wood and has a private deck and oversized tub.

Decorated in pretty, blue tones, Room 2 is furnished with antiques, tiled fireplace, and tub for two. Rooms 8 and 9, located on the ground floor of a fourplex cottage, have fire-

places and outdoor decks. Rooms 10 and 11 on the second floor have corner fireplaces and oversized tubs.

Rooms here range from the low $100 range to the low $200 range.

GLENDEVEN

8221 North Highway 1
Little River, CA 95456
Telephone: (707) 937-0083

Ten rooms, each with private bath; eight with fireplaces and bay views. Breakfast is served at your door
in a basket or on a tray. Smoking is not permitted. No
handicapped access. Moderate to deluxe.

Getting There
From San Francisco, take Highway 101 north past
Cloverdale. Drive west on Highway 128 to Highway 1.
The inn is a half mile north of Little River and two
miles south of Mendocino on
Highway 1.

GLENDEVEN

Little River

We pulled into the quiet burg of Little River on one of those sunny, spring afternoons that make you want to call the office and quit your job. After checking into your room at Glendeven, you might even be tempted to sell the house and move north. Luckily (or maybe to protect guests from crazy impulses), there aren't any phones at Glendeven.

We found the inn's own brochure description of a "handsome farmhouse" a considerable understatement. Expecting a typically quaint bed and breakfast, we were pleasantly surprised at the spaciousness and diversity of accommodations at this coastal retreat. As a couple of travelers well-seasoned in sleuthing out places of the heart, we found Glendeven to be unsurpassed in romantic perfection.

Rooms for Romance

True, there is a handsome farmhouse. The Garrett, a charming attic room with dormer windows (low $100 range), faces the bay. The Eastlin Suite, also under the main house's roof, offers a sitting room, fireplace, bay view through French doors, and a rosewood, queen-sized bed.

But the refurbished farmhouse comprises only a part of Glendeven. There are two other buildings housing delightful guest quarters. The Barnhouse Suite used to be an old hay barn until the inn's owners reconstructed it as their private residence. They have since moved off the property and made the suite available to guests. Priced at around $200 (higher rate for four people), it comes complete with two bedrooms, handcrafted wood furniture, and stereo system. An art gallery comprises the barn's ground floor.

Our favorite spot was Stevenscroft, a remote, four-room annex situated at the rear of the property. Upstairs, the high-ceilinged Briar Rose room (mid $100 range) overlooked the gardens and was decorated in French Country.

We were lucky enough to score Pinewood (mid $100 range), located on the lower level of Stevenscroft. The decor was a workable mix of country and playful, with art ranging from beautiful quilts displayed on the wall and a copper weathervane to a wooden wedge of watermelon (partially eaten) and a suspended birdcage containing an oversized, stuffed parrot. French doors opened onto a private deck, and a cozy nook with daybed afforded a sweeping view to the distant bay. The wood arranged neatly in the fireplace awaited only a match.

On our first afternoon here, visions of a walk through nearby Fern Canyon, a stroll on the beach, and a picnic on the lawn outside were among our well-intentioned diversion options. But the room's romantic magic kept us indoors. (After all, how often do working parents of young children find themselves alone in such splendor?)

Apparently, we weren't the only couple to be lulled by Glendeven's sensual charms. (No, we didn't count notches on the bedpost.) A double-volume diary described the rendezvous of scores of previous Pinewood guests. Skimming through the entries we paused at one particularly intriguing account of a visit by Chuck and Patty. Several pages (and only a couple of months) later, we found another Chuck and Patty entry—with even greater raves. Maybe Glendeven is better the second time around.

The Headlands Inn

Corner of Howard and Albion streets
(P.O. Box 132), Mendocino, CA 95460
Telephone: (707) 937-4431

Five rooms, each with private bath and fireplace.
Amenities include afternoon tea and cookies, morning
newspaper, bathrobes (in some rooms), fresh flowers,
and extra pillows in guest rooms. Fresh fruit and sweets
served in upstairs parlor. Breakfast with hot entree
(delivered to room) included. Two-night minimum stay
during weekends; three-or-four-night minimum stay
during holidays. Smoking is not permitted.
Handicapped access. Moderate to expensive.

Getting There
From San Francisco, take Highway 101 north past
Cloverdale. Drive west on Highway 128 to Highway 1.
From Highway 1 in Mendocino, turn left at business
district exit and right from Lansing onto Howard
Street. Inn is one and a half blocks on left.

HEADLANDS INN

Mendocino

*D*on't let the fact that the Headlands Inn has a downtown location scare you away. With not a single stoplight except on the highway and a main street that's only about four blocks long, Mendocino isn't exactly wrought with noise and congestion. Unless, of course, you count the crashing surf and circling seagulls as noise and congestion.

The inn, which began life as John Barry's barbershop in 1868, has since served stints as a restaurant, hotel annex, and, more recently, as a private residence. Sharon and David Hyman bought the building recently and upgraded the five cozy guest rooms. All have woodburning fireplaces and feature a mix of antiques, reproductions, and contemporary furnishings.

Rooms for Romance

The largest room in the house is the Bessie Strauss (high $100 range) on the second floor. An antique pie crust-styled table and two wooden chairs sit before a lace-draped bay window that overlooks the English garden to the ocean, offering guests a great spot for breakfast (delivered to your room). A king-sized bed, Victorian-style sofa, and sitting area complete the setting.

Guests in the third-floor John Barry Room (mid $100 range) can relax under a gabled ceiling or curl up on the dormer window love seat. The queen-sized feather bed sits under the brightly papered eaves. This room commands a spectacular ocean view.

The centerpiece of the W.J. Wilson Room (low $100 range) is a woodburning stove on a raised hearth. A private deck is just outside.

For privacy seekers, the Casper Cottage (low to mid $100 range) is detached from the main house and comes complete with a small refrigerator, perfect for chilling a bottle of bubbly. The cottage is furnished with a four-poster, queen-sized bed, antique armoire, two overstuffed chairs, and an extra-long tub (bubblebath included).

JOSHUA GRINDLE INN

44800 Little Lake Road
(P.O. Box 647), Mendocino, CA 95460
Telephone: (707) 937-4143

Ten rooms, each with private bath; six with fireplaces. Breakfast included. Two-night minimum
during holidays. Limited handicapped access.
Smoking is not permitted. Moderate.

Getting There
From the Bay Area, follow Highway 101 past
Cloverdale; west on Highway 128 and north on
Highway 1. In Mendocino, turn left at Little Lake
Road (stoplight); inn is on the right. Driving time
from San Francisco via Highway 101 is approxi-
mately three and a half hours; the trip up twisting
Highway 1 takes five hours.

JOSHUA GRINDLE INN

Mendocino

*I*n this quaint community, where bed-and-breakfast inns are as plentiful as seagulls, the Joshua Grindle is a standout. Framed by a white picket fence and the bluest of California skies (when the fog's not around, that is), Mr. Grindle's old Victorian homestead is quintessential Mendocino. Situated on a pretty knoll a short stroll from downtown, the inn has for many years ranked among the most popular along the north coast.

Rooms for Romance

Half the rooms (all have private baths) are located in the main house, built over a hundred years ago by the inn's namesake, a town banker. The Grindle, Joshua's bedroom, offers an ocean and bay view, while the Master has a fireplace and a view of the garden and trees. Both feature queen beds and sitting areas.

The Cypress Cottage and Watertower buildings set privately at the rear of the grounds were our personal favorites. Our room for the night occupied most of the ground floor of the tower, a replica (complete with inward-sloping walls) of the many vintage watertowers that dot the community. The spacious room was furnished in comfortable early American with an antique magazine rack in the shape of the tower. A small woodburning stove sat on a corner brick hearth with wood stacked neatly in a tiny, antique wheelbarrow.

Watertower II on the second floor was similarly furnished, although it offered a nicer city view with a peek of the ocean. Cypress North, part of the adjacent, two-unit Cypress Cottage and a favorite among returning guests, also featured cozy early American and a fireplace. Both cottage rooms have beamed, cathedral ceilings. Most rooms are offered in the low $100 range.

At breakfast, innkeepers Jim and Arlene Moorehead do a nice job of making guests comfortable as everyone gathers for homemade goodies at the antique pine harvest table in the kitchen.

Stanford Inn by the Sea

Coast Highway and Comptche-Ukiah Road
(P.O. Box 487), Mendocino, CA 95460
Telephone: (707) 937-5615

Twenty-six rooms and suites, each with private bath
and robes. Continental breakfast included. Two-
night minimum stay on weekends. Smoking is not
permitted. No handicapped access. Moderate to
deluxe.

Getting There
From San Francisco, take Highway 101 north past
Cloverdale. Drive west on Highway 128 to
Highway 1. The inn is just off Highway 1 at the
mouth of Big River on the outskirts of Mendocino.

STANFORD INN BY THE SEA

Mendocino

hile preparing the first edition of this book, we heard that innkeepers Jeff and Joan Stanford had done wonders with an aging, motel-style lodge overlooking Mendocino Bay. After a personal visit, however, the term miracles seemed more appropriate. And the miracles continue.

While others might have torn down the existing structure and started fresh, Jeff, as if following some divine vision, began making extraordinary improvements that continue, even years later. The result is one of the region's most charming country inns—inside and out.

If you enjoy the out-of-doors, there are acres of landscaped and wild grounds to explore, gardens to tour, and even llamas to pet. A greenhouse-enclosed swimming pool, spa, and sauna are also on site. In addition, the inn offers an assortment of quality mountain bikes and

canoe rentals on Big River, a short walk from your room.

For those not motivated to wander, views of the grounds, llamas, and more can be had from the comfort of your own deck. And there are plenty of additional niceties—besides each other—to keep you occupied.

No expense has been spared in creature comforts here. Rooms are paneled in tasteful pine and are furnished with four-poster king or queen beds with down comforters and pillows. All have fireplaces or wood stoves, refrigerators, and French doors, and are stocked with complimentary coffee, chocolate truffles, and local wine, in addition to a selection of shampoos, conditioners, lotions, etc.

In recent years Jeff and Joan have gutted most of the bathrooms and installed new fixtures and tub-and-shower combinations.

Wait. There's more. Each room has a remote-controlled television and video cassette recorder as well as a stereo radio/cassette/compact disc player. (Don't forget to bring mood music.)

Rooms for Romance

While the decor varies slightly throughout the inn, you can't go wrong with any of the twenty-six rooms. However, some accommodations have more dramatic views than others. For the best views of Mendocino village and bay, ask for Rooms 7, 8, 9, 10, 11, or 12 on the lower floor or Rooms 23, 24, 25, or 26 on the upper floor. The upper-floor rooms offer more private decks.

Rooms range from the mid to upper $100 range. Suites command rates from around $200 to the mid $200 range.

BENBOW INN

445 Lake Benbow Drive
Garberville, CA 95440
Telephone: (707) 923-2124

Fifty-five rooms, each with private bath; three with
fireplaces. Complimentary English tea and scones
served each afternoon and complimentary hors d'oeuvres each evening. Movies shown daily. Restaurant.
Golf, swimming, and boating nearby. Closed January
through March. Smoking is not permitted. No handicapped access. Moderate to deluxe.

Getting There
From San Francisco, follow Highway 101 north for
approximately 240 miles (about a four-hour drive).
Two miles south of Garberville, exit Highway 101 at
Lake Benbow Drive. Inn is adjacent to highway.

BENBOW INN

Garberville

*A*fter miles and miles of tortuous twisting and turning along Highways 1 and 101, the Benbow Inn emerges through the trees as an oasis: the proverbial pot of gold.

Built in an era when remote resort hotels were still considered destinations, the 1920s-era Benbow Inn attracted guests who stayed for days—even weeks—enjoying golf, fishing, swimming, and boating. The inn offered vacationers all the trappings of a world-class resort, only on a smaller scale.

While other establishments of those days have gone to seed, the years have been kinder to the Benbow Inn. Owners Chuck and Patsy Watts have in recent years continued to pump new life into the Tudor-style structure, adding modern conveniences as well as new rooms, all while preserving the grace and charm of old.

Rooms for Romance

Wanting to view as many rooms as possible, we wisely dropped by during a winter shutdown. Otherwise most, if not all, the best rooms would have been occupied.

Actually, best rooms is a misnomer of sorts, since you really can't go wrong with any of

the accommodations at this National Historic Landmark. Wandering down the halls, however, a few did stand out. Room 206, for example, featured a mood-inspiring red scheme with dark woods, English-style decor, four-poster bed, and shuttered windows.

Our favorite was Room 119, a newer cottage room off the patio. This enormous room held a grandfather clock, eight-foot-tall hutch, wing chairs, fireplace, wet bar, and writing desk, all under a pitched, beamed ceiling. Even after all of this there was still enough room for a canopied, king-sized bed.

The bathroom, a work of sensual art, held a Jacuzzi tub with mood lighting, separate shower, and double sinks. A private deck overlooked the Eel River flowing just outside.

Many rooms are available for less than $100 per night. More deluxe accommodations are offered in the low to high $100 range. Only the Garden Cottage is over $200.

GINGERBREAD MANSION

400 Berding Street
Ferndale, CA 95536
Telephone: (707) 786-4000

Nine rooms and suites, each with private bath; four
with fireplaces. Amenities include bathrobes, bubblebath, bedside chocolate truffles, and afternoon
tea and cake. The inn also provides free use of bicycles and even rubber boots and umbrellas for those
rainy days. Continental breakfast served in dining
room; coffee, tea, or juice left outside the rooms
before breakfast. Two-night minimum on weekends
and during holiday periods. Limited handicapped
access. Smoking is not permitted. Moderate to
expensive.

Getting There
From Highway 101, fifteen miles south of Eureka,
take Fernbridge/Ferndale exit; five miles to Main
Street; turn left at the blue bank building, one block
to inn.

Gingerbread Mansion

Ferndale

*J*ust when we thought we'd seen most every romantic guest amenity, someone suggested the Gingerbread Mansion and its toe-to-toe tubs. The idea for this creative bathing experience was hatched in the inn's Rose Suite, equipped with a single clawfoot tub and mirrored wall and ceiling. Upon seeing the double reflection, guests began suggesting that two might be better than one. Innkeeper Ken Torbert listened, and the rest is history.

Even if you haven't visited the Gingerbread Mansion in Ferndale, chances are you've seen its photograph. The fabled peach-and-yellow Victorian façade has been pictured countless times in guidebooks, travel magazines, and architectural publications throughout the nation. However, this ornate manse—not to mention the twin tubs—has to be savored in person to be fully appreciated.

Rooms for Romance

In the Fountain Suite (high $100 range), two tubs are placed side-by-side at the center of a spacious bathroom that also features a tiled fireplace and chaise longue. And since you can't spend all your time soaking, there's a queen-sized bed with bonnet canopy and a view of the garden and village from the bay window.

Across the hall, the Rose Suite (high $100 range) features a bedroom-sized bathroom complete with bidet and fireplace. In the bedroom, strategically placed mirrors around the ceiling rosette provide you both with a view of a second fireplace—from the comfort of your bed.

Our room, the Gingerbread Suite (mid $100 range), held toe-to-toe tubs, placed on a raised platform behind a white Victorian railing. This spacious room, with queen-sized bed and multiple, coordinating wallpapers, is situated on the main floor just off the dining room.

The Garden Room (mid $100 range), also on the main floor, is situated just off the luscious private garden and features French windows, lace curtains, corner fireplace, and queen-sized bed.

"The Original House" at The Carter House

1033 Third Street
Eureka, CA 95501
Telephone: (707) 445-1390

Seven rooms and suites, each with private bath; two with fireplaces; two with spa tubs for two. Breakfast with hot entree included. Late afternoon and evening cordial hour also provided. Dining room across the street at "The Inn." Smoking is not permitted. Handicapped access. Moderate to deluxe.

Getting There
From Highway 101 in downtown Eureka, west on L Street through Old Town to hotel.

"The Original House" at The Carter House

*E*ureka native son, Mark Carter, grew up enamored with the work of Joseph Newsom, designer of the city's landmark Carson Mansion, considered by many to be the nation's finest example of Victorian architecture. In fact, Mark was so impressed that after discovering an old Newsom-designed Victorian house plan, he replicated it for his own family—within sight of the famous Carson Mansion.

Over a two-year period, Mark and a three-person crew built the imposing, four-story, redwood manor themselves, following the architect's every original minute detail, down to dual marble fireplaces and triple parlors on the main floor. However, Mark, his wife Christie, and their children soon felt overwhelmed by the size of their mansion, and made the decision to convert the still-new structure into a first-class country inn.

Rooms for Romance

The Carters' former living area on the second floor has become the inn's showplace suite (high $100 range) featuring a fireplace, extra bedroom, and a bright and cheery bathroom with tiled floor and oak trim, as well as spa tub for two. There's also a communal kitchen on the second floor where coffee is available.

On the third floor is the Burgundy Room (mid $100 range), actually a suite with a king-sized, canopied bed and private bath with a tub and shower combination. The oft-photographed Carson Mansion is visible from this suite. A harbor view is available from a gable window in the Blue Room next door.

There are two rooms on the inn's lower level. One of these, the Striped Room (low $100 range), has its own bath down the hall. This is the least expensive room.

Rooms are decorated with Oriental rugs, fresh flowers, original art, flannel robes, and fluffy comforters.

Breakfast, an afterthought at many bed-and-breakfast inns, is a masterpiece at the Carter House. Among the changing specialties are delicate tarts, smoked salmon, and eggs benedict, along with fruit dishes, muffins, and fresh juices.

"The Inn" at The Carter House

301 L Street
Eureka, CA 95501
Telephone: (707) 444-8062

Twenty-three rooms and suites, each with private bath,
telephone, and television; six with fireplaces; four with
spa tubs for two. Breakfast with hot entree and homemade
muffins and tarts included. Late afternoon and evening
cordial hour also provided. Dining room. Smoking is not
permitted. Handicapped access. Moderate to deluxe.

Getting There
From Highway 101 in downtown Eureka, west on
L Street through Old Town to hotel.

"THE INN" AT THE CARTER HOUSE

Eureka

*N*o, it's not coincidence that the two hostelries sitting on opposite corners in Old Town Eureka bear the Carter name. Mark Carter built the twenty-room, Victorian-style inn after converting his own grand home across the street into a successful small bed-and-breakfast inn (see previous listing). These two properties, along with a cottage, form The Carter House.

Modeled after a nineteenth-century Eureka hotel, the inn bears the same attention to detail as the Carters' "Original House." Everything, from construction detailing and furnishings to the nationally recognized hotel restaurant, is first class.

While the Carters' "Original House" represents a total escape from everyday hustle and bustle, the inn is more connected to the pulse of life. Although rooms are furnished with handsome English pine antiques and cozy fireplaces, they're also equipped with contemporary conveniences like phones and televisions.

Rooms for Romance

Since our first visit, Mark has created a selection of romantic suites under the eaves on the inn's third floor. These are furnished with queen-sized beds, original art, marble fireplaces, sitting areas, and entertainment centers with televisions, videocassette players, and compact disc players. These suites are also romantically equipped with oversized, double-head showers and whirlpool tubs for two.

Our suite, #302, held a step-up, thirty-two-inch-deep spa tub for two under a window with views of the marina, the Carson Mansion, and the nearby Victorian Pink Lady, a local landmark. The queen-sized bed was placed nearby. A sitting room with a tiled, woodburning fire-

place and couch was separated from the sleeping chamber by French doors. The bathroom was equipped with an oversized shower with spigots for each of you. The third-floor suites are offered in the low $200 range.

Priced in the high $100 range are two second-floor suites equipped with single-sized whirlpool tubs. One of these, room 201, commands a view of the marina and the Pink Lady. The room also has a windowseat and a fireplace.

Down the hall, Room 204 (mid $100 range) holds a queen-sized bed and single-sized spa tub. This room offers a view of the Carson Mansion.

On the inn's first floor are several standard rooms and the Carters' dining room, one of the finest in the Pacific Northwest.

THE WINE COUNTRY

Daytime Diversions

After you've visited a few of the more famous wineries of the valley, turn off onto some of the less traveled roads and visit a small winery or two. One of our favorites is Chateau Montelena on Tubbs Lane off Highway 29, outside of Calistoga. Walk around back for a look at the winery's medieval-style façade. While you're there, take a look at the spectacular oriental garden complete with lake, tea houses, and an old Chinese junk.

For a different view of the valley, the Napa Valley Wine Train makes brunch and dinner runs along Highway 29. A number of companies offer early morning balloon flights over the valley floor. Your hotel/inn staff can provide names of operators.

The quaint community of Calistoga is home to several spas and hot springs where you can get a soothing mud bath and massage.

Tables for Two

Silverado Resort (Atlas Peak Road, Napa) features the best fresh seafood buffet we've ever sampled. Auberge du Soleil (Rutherford Hill Road) serves highly acclaimed meals with a view of the valley. A personal favorite is Tra Vigne (along Highway 29, St. Helena), offering memorable Italian specialties in a convivial, European atmosphere. Mustard's Grill (Highway 29, Yountville), despite its fame, remains one of the valley's best. Bistro Don Giovanni (formerly Table 29) on Highway 29 in Napa opened in 1993 to positive reviews. Showley's on Adams Street in St. Helena was recommended by more than one of our inkeeping hosts.

In the Sonoma wine country area, Madrona Manor offers an excellent fixed-price dinner menu and wine list.

After Hours

The Napa Valley is pretty quiet after nightfall. However, if you'd like to enjoy an evening out, the deco-styled lounge at the Mount View Hotel on Calistoga's main street usually offers soft, live music. The lounge at Auberge du Soleil offers panoramic evening vistas and wine by the glass.

Auberge du Soleil

180 Rutherford Hill Road
Rutherford, CA 94573
Telephone: (707) 963-1211

Twenty-nine rooms and nineteen suites, each with
private bath, fireplace, tub for two, and videocassette
player. Complimentary candy and fruit placed in
room upon arrival. Amenities include fresh flowers in
rooms, double-sheeted beds, bathrobes, bubblebath
gel, in-room refrigerators and honor bars. Round-the-
clock room service, videocassette movie library,
swimming pool/spa (heated year-round and open
round the clock), steam sauna, exercise room, beauty
salon, tennis courts with staff pro, and massage service available. Award-winning restaurant. Two-night
minimum stay on weekends. Reservations for the
most popular rooms advised six to twelve months in
advance. Smoking is allowed. Handicapped access.
Deluxe.

Getting There
From Interstate 80, take Highway 29 north past
Napa. Drive east on Route 128 at Rutherford; turn left
on the Silverado Trail and then make an immediate
right on Rutherford Hill Road, to resort.

AUBERGE DU SOLEIL

Rutherford

*A*fter checking in at Auberge du Soleil one winter afternoon, we hurried to our private deck to savor a couple of rare hours of warm sunshine. While such a lazy afternoon would typically invite a sprinkling of fairy dust, the Napa Valley scene beyond—mustard-coated vineyards, wineries, and rolling hills—kept our eyes wide until the sun slipped behind the hills.

This French-styled full-service inn, set on a wooded hillside just off the Silverado Trail, is one of few wine-country inns that afford panoramic valley vistas. And Auberge du Soleil was built with the view in mind. Its forty-eight rooms are spread among eleven cottages over thirty-three acres. All have private, spacious decks overlooking Napa Valley and the hills beyond.

On our visit, we were treated to a sampling of sun and showers, each creating a different, pleasant atmosphere. In the morning, hot air balloons floated above a dreamy valley mist.

Rooms for Romance

The cottages, each named after a French province, are set above and below a long drive-way. The lower units—Versailles, Provence, Normandie, Armagnac, Lorraine, Picardie, and Alsace—offer unobstructed valley views and the most privacy. Rooms are styled throughout in comfortable Mediterranean/Southwest decor and Mexican pavers. Covered patio decks are private enough for lounging in the white, terry robes provided in each room.

Rates at Auberge du Soleil range from the lower $300 range to over $800 per night.

Our room, Versailles Eight (high $300 range), had a deluxe, king-sized bed. It overlooked the valley and the resort's championship tennis courts. We particularly enjoyed having the fireplace positioned near our bed. Versailles One, a one-bedroom suite, is another oft-requested room.

The bathrooms at Auberge du Soleil merit particular mention. Each has a large dual tub (Jacuzzi tubs in deluxe rooms) illuminated by a skylight. Some even boast sexy, tiled showers with double shower heads.

Among the more recent additions to the inn's grounds is a half-mile-long sculpture trail with picnic areas.

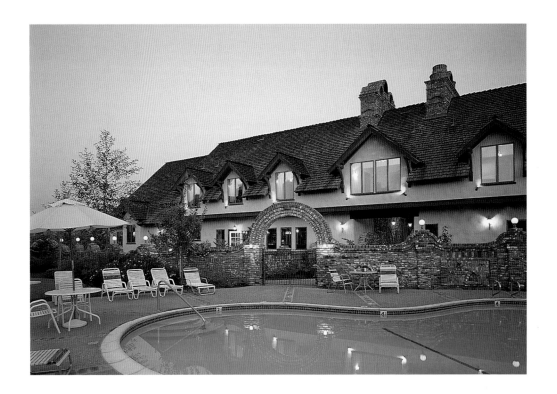

HARVEST INN

One Main Street
St. Helena, CA 94574
Telephone: (707) 963-WINE

Fifty-five rooms, forty-eight with fireplaces, three
with tubs for two. Two swimming pools/spas.
Continental breakfast. Complimentary snacks in
lobby. Wine and beer bar. Bicycle rentals. Smoking is
allowed in some areas. Handicapped access.
Moderate to deluxe.

Getting There
From Interstate 80, take Highway 29 north past Napa
to St. Helena. The inn is at the edge of town on
Highway 29, which is also Main Street.

HARVEST INN

St. Helena

Queen of Hearts, Count of Fantasy, Earl of Ecstasy... With names like these, it's clear the creators of Harvest Inn weren't designing rooms with sleeping in mind. Not that you won't get a good night's sleep here. It's just that there are so many other, er, things to do.

One of the more innocent—although pleasant—pastimes at Harvest Inn is a stroll around the grounds. Clusters of Tudor-style pods set among seven colorful, lush acres give the feeling of an English village. The intricate brick and stonework found along the walkways and chimneys were featured in Smithsonian magazine. (Cobblestone from an old San Francisco street was used to build the fireplace in the inn's library.)

The use of brick is carried into the guest rooms, where expansive fireplaces are common. In Count of Fantasy, empty wine bottles left by former guests adorn the wall-length fireplace.

Rooms for Romance

Lord of the Manor is the inn's ultimate accommodation. The sumptuous split-level suite, located in the handsome Harvest Manor House, has a fireplace on each level, wool carpeting, and a cozy, oak-paneled reading nook. The bedroom, found on the upper level, is equipped with a spacious spa tub and shower. Lady of the Manor and Knight of Nights, two adjacent suites, are similarly styled. All three carry weekend rates in the $300-per-night range.

Count of Fantasy, another deluxe room with private patio, is decorated with pecan paneling, Persian rugs, wet bar, and fireplace. The Beaujolais Room is billed as perfect for a "honeymoon couple on a budget." Inside are a king-sized bed, fireplace, and wet bar. The inn's in-ground spa is just outside. The weekend rate for this room is in the low $100 range.

Our room, Chianti, was a large, oak-plank-floored room furnished with antiques. A floor-to-ceiling fireplace rounded one of the corners. (Wood was stacked outside.) A tug on the drapery sash of the sliding glass door revealed a private patio and view of the inn-owned Cabernet vineyard and the Mayacamas Mountains beyond.

Harvest Inn occupies a prime spot of vineland just south of St. Helena. With neighbors like Sutter Home Winery and Prager Port Works, guests are never far away from Napa Valley fun.

Meadowood Resort Hotel

900 Meadowood Lane
St. Helena, CA 94574
Telephone: (707) 963-3646

Eighty-two rooms, suites, and lodges, each with private bath and deck; most have fireplaces. Amenities include comforters, bathrobes, bubblebath, and honor-bar refrigerators. Restaurants and bar. Health spa equipped with whirlpool, lap pool, massage rooms, and exercise equipment. Tennis courts, swimming pool, golf course, and croquet lawn. Smoking is permitted. Handicapped access. Deluxe.

Getting There
From Interstate 80, take Highway 29 north past Napa to St. Helena. In St. Helena, turn right on Pope Street. At the Silverado Trail, turn left; then make an immediate right on Howell Mountain Road; follow for 100 yards and turn left on Meadowood Lane.

MEADOWOOD RESORT HOTEL

St. Helena

*W*e may be hard-pressed to describe last night's dinner, but our first visit to Meadowood several years ago remains a vivid, pleasant memory. Flaming crimson vineyards against a crisp, fall blue sky; nattily dressed croquet players; the deer foraging outside our window...

Meadowood has been a Napa Valley favorite of ours for years, yet it continues to elude many. Tucked discreetly behind trees just above the Silverado Trail, the resort resists calling overt attention to itself. It's not marked by neon nor by any other conspicuous sign; you'll know you've arrived when you reach the security guard post. From there, the road winds through the woods, past clusters of cottages, the swimming pool, and tennis courts.

While many hostelries offer only a few rooms that are eminently conducive to romance, we haven't discovered accommodations at Meadowood that didn't measure up to our lovers' list of criteria.

Rooms for Romance

On our first visit we chanced to spend two nights in one of several freestanding hillside cottages near the entrance to the property. Our very private hideaway had a separate sitting room with woodburning stove and well-stocked refrigerator. The bedroom, bright and spacious, opened onto a private deck. Because our bungalow sat above the rest at the end of a private walkway, our only visitors were a few curious deer.

More contemporary suites are available in the resort's central area. These feature cathedral ceilings and skylights, and many have stone fireplaces. All accommodations at Meadowood are equipped with comforters, bathrobes, bubblebath, refrigerators, and blow dryers. Nightly rates at Meadowood range from the high $200 range to around $600.

Although the vastness of Meadowood can at first seem a bit intimidating (we followed a golfcart-driving bellman to our remote cottage), the wooded walkways and twisting lanes shed their mystery after a leisurely, get-acquainted stroll around the grounds.

At the northern end of the property is one of California's preeminent croquet lawns. The sight of well-heeled gentry, resplendent in crisp whites, playing in the shadow of Meadowood's Cape Cod architecture, makes for a stunning, Gatsby-like scene, particularly on a sunny day.

If you left your mallets at home, tennis and swimming facilities are available at Meadowood. Guests may also choose from two on-site restaurants and a cozy lounge.

Wine Country Inn

1152 Lodi Lane
St. Helena, CA 94574
Telephone: (707) 963-7077

Twenty-five rooms, each with private bath; fifteen
with fireplaces. Continental breakfast included.
Swimming pool and spa. Smoking is allowed. No
handicapped access. Moderate to deluxe.

Getting There
From Interstate 80, take Highway 29 north past Napa
to St. Helena. Two miles north of St. Helena, turn
east on Lodi Lane; inn is on the left.

WINE COUNTRY INN

St. Helena

*I*f you're a first-time visitor to Napa Valley, don't be discouraged by the anonymous, cookie-cutter hotels that seem to be proliferating faster than grapevines. There thankfully are a few recently constructed hostelries that evoke the all-but-abandoned charm and character of yesteryear. The Wine Country Inn represents a pleasing blend of old and new.

The manor house is an appealing hybrid of various styles. Although classic New England styling is evident, flourishes like the fieldstone walls were definitely inspired by historic area wineries.

The inn sits atop a hill surrounded by manicured gardens, trees, lawn, and vineyards. A swimming pool and spa (for those blistering Napa Valley summers) are located downslope from the main building.

Rooms for Romance

Like the exterior, guest rooms here draw some inspiration from the inns of old, with country-style furnishings, homespun quilts, and iron beds. Welcome contemporary touches include patios, balconies, wet bars, and modern bathrooms. Accommodations at the Wine Country Inn are so varied that during our last visit about eight different rates were listed from around $100 to just over $200.

One of the nicest rooms is Room 24, comprising the entire floor of Hastings House, one of the peripheral buildings. The room has a four-poster, queen-sized bed, fireplace, balcony, a spa tub for two, and an alcove with its own daybed.

In Brandy Barn, a cottage unit, Room 17 has a queen-sized bed, small sitting room, and balcony. Room 22 has a fireplace and balcony. Both overlook a neighboring vineyard toward majestic Glass Mountain.

Room 9, located on the third floor of the main house, has both eastern and southern exposures and offers views of vineyards and mountains, as well as the lawn and pool area. Besides the inn's best view, Room 9 features a fireplace and balcony.

Country Meadow Inn

11360 Old Redwood Highway
Windsor, CA 95492
Telephone: (707) 431-1276

Five rooms, each with private bath; three with fireplaces. Breakfast with hot entree included. Smoking is
not permitted. Handicapped access. Moderate to
expensive.

Getting There
Exit Highway 101 at Healdsburg Avenue in Windsor,
about sixty miles north of San Francisco. Turn left;
road becomes Old Redwood Highway; follow for
nearly two miles; inn is on the left just past Piper
Sonoma Cellars.

COUNTRY MEADOW INN

Windsor

*W*ith rates for a romantic room that peak at just over $100, Country Meadow Inn is one of the wine country's best bargains—and best-kept secrets. What's more, there's no catch.

The inn's reasonable rates are not based on any lack of service or amenities (Country Meadow is as appealing as most inns), but more likely its location in a community not widely known as a getaway destination. Truth is, Windsor really is a great place to get away from it all.

Rooms for Romance

What better place to savor the rural set-ting than the Garden Suite (mid $100 range). Guests lucky enough to snare this retreat (the only guestroom on the ground floor) are indulged with an atrium, a king-sized, canopied bed, oak antiques, wicker furnishings, touches of lace, a fire-place, and a spacious bath with a whirlpool tub for two.

On the second floor of this Queen Anne Victorian, the Mahogany Room (around $100) has a tiled fireplace and an ornate, queen-sized mahogany bed bedecked with a soft satin and lace com-forter.

The Woodrose Room (low $100 range) is illuminated by bay windows and also features a fireplace and larger-than-king-sized bed with down comforter.

Belle de Jour Inn

16276 Healdsburg Avenue
Healdsburg, CA 95448
Telephone: (707) 431-7412

Four cottage rooms, each with private bath, refrigerator, and fireplace or woodburning stove; two rooms
have whirlpool tubs for two. Amenities include fresh
flowers and robes. Full breakfast included. Three-
night minimum stay during all major holidays.
Smoking is not permitted. Handicapped access.
Moderate to expensive.

Getting There

From northbound Highway 101, drive past
Healdsburg and exit at Dry Creek Road. Turn right
on Dry Creek Road and left at the stoplight on
Healdsburg Avenue. Drive one mile on Healdsburg
Avenue (you'll see Simi Winery on your left) and
turn right up the tree-lined drive to inn.

BELLE DE JOUR INN

Healdsburg

*L*ooking for a romantic destination where you and your partner can savor a cozy cottage for two? Your search ends at Belle de Jour, a six-acre retreat on the outskirts of Healdsburg.

An Italianate-styled Victorian, home of innkeepers Tom and Brenda Hearn, presides over this compound of four tidy cottages, each equipped with the modern niceties needed for your romantic getaway. The beds are even covered in crisp sheets dried by the sun.

Rooms for Romance

Our room of choice was the Terrace Room (high $100 range), which holds a king-sized brass bed and a fireplace. A big spa tub for the two of you sits under a window overlooking your private raised deck and an expanse of rolling tree-studded countryside beyond. Roses bloom out front.

The Caretaker's Suite is another favorite. A king-sized bed dominates one end of this spacious room with hardwood floors and sitting area with wicker furniture. A Franklin fireplace is close enough to warm your toes under the sheets. This room, which also has a whirlpool tub for two with a view and a separate shower, is priced in the mid $100 range.

Atelier is a large sunny studio with a vaulted ceiling, woodburning stove, a queen-sized, canopied bed, and a whirlpool tub for one. The Morning Hill Room has a French door entry, a queen-sized bed, and a shower and steam unit in the bathroom. These two rooms are offered in the low $100 range.

Each morning, guests are invited into Tom and Brenda's Victorian for breakfast. Later in the day, the two (or four) of you might want to schedule a romantic, chauffeured backroad or winery tour in the innkeepers' classic 1925 Star automobile.

CAMELLIA INN

211 North Street
Healdsburg, CA 95448
Telephone: (707) 433-8182

Nine rooms, seven with private baths. Four rooms
have gas fireplaces. Amenities include fresh flowers
and extra pillows with satin pillowcases. Swimming
pool. Full breakfast included. Two-night minimum if
Saturday night stay desired. Smoking is not permitted. Limited handicapped access. Moderate.

Getting There
Healdsburg is sixty-five miles north of San Francisco
on Highway 101. Leave Highway 101 at Central
Healdsburg exit. Go north on Healdsburg Avenue;
turn right on North Street, two blocks to inn.

CAMELLIA INN

Healdsburg

Camellia Inn, a century-old Italianate Victorian townhouse, takes its name from the more than two-dozen different varieties of camellias that dot the grounds. (The colorful bushes are thought to have been planted by noted horticulturist Luther Burbank, a friend of early owners.) The abundant flowers, however, are but one of this graceful inn's many attributes, the most appealing of which are behind closed doors.

Rooms for Romance

Firelight is among the most appealing of the nine rooms. Features include a silk-screened frieze, antique armoire, Oriental rug, and canopied, queen-sized bed. The room's bay window faces the shaded front of the house. Firelight has a private entrance.

Two particularly decadent rooms are Tower Room East and Tower Room West. These have been added more recently, and both offer gas fireplaces, dual spa tubs, and queen-sized beds. Tower West is equipped with a ceiling fan. Both carry very reasonable rates of around $125.

A final note: If indoor activities at Camellia Inn leave you with sufficient energy, consider walking to Healdsburg's quaint town plaza, just two blocks away.

MADRONA MANOR

1001 Westside Road
Healdsburg, CA 95448
Telephone: (707) 433-4231

Twenty-one rooms and suites, each with private bath;
eighteen with fireplaces. Swimming pool. Award-win-
ning restaurant. European-style breakfast included.
Modified American plan available on request.
Smoking is not permitted. Handicapped access.
Moderate to deluxe.

Getting There
Healdsburg is sixty-five miles north of San Francisco
on Highway 101. Take the Central Healdsburg exit
at Westside Road and drive west to inn.

MADRONA MANOR

Healdsburg

*I*t's difficult to believe (for this working couple, anyway) that the three-story elegance of Madrona Manor was intended originally to be enjoyed only as a summer retreat. Although wealthy San Francisco businessman John Paxton enjoyed the mansion for a time, the home actually stood vacant for nearly half its hundred years, until 1981. That's when John and Carol Muir arrived on the scene with visions of creating an inn. The couple's diligence has paid dividends as Madrona Manor has emerged as one of Northern California's preeminent country inns.

The buildings are spread over eight landscaped acres. Offering a total of twenty-one rooms and suites, the inn is large compared to many of its Victorian counterparts. Nine guest rooms are found in the manor house, with the rest housed in the Carriage House (nine rooms; six with fireplaces), Meadow Wood complex (two suites), and the Garden Suite.

Rooms for Romance

Wedding nights are often spent in Room 101 on the first floor of the mansion. This room is equipped with a canopied double bed. The bathroom has a large clawfoot tub.

The two beautiful, front-facing rooms off the mansion's second-floor balcony are Rooms 203 and 204 (upper $100 range). Among the inn's most popular, they still contain original furniture, including cozy double beds, from the mansion's early years. Room 204 was the

bedroom of the original owner and features a sunny bay window overlooking the garden. Both have antique clawfoot tubs, fireplaces, and spacious sitting areas, and each has access to the large balcony. We do not recommend Rooms 301 or 302 for a romantic getaway.

More modern decor is found in the Garden Suite (around $200), a spacious and secluded retreat equipped with a marble fireplace, tub for two, and private deck.

Room 401 in the Carriage House has a rate in the low $100 range and is a favorite among lovers on a budget. The ultra-decadent Suite 400 in the Carriage House features a fireplace, private deck, and spa tub for two in a bath of Grecian marble. The fireplace is visible from the tub through shutters. Suite 400 is offered in the low $200 range.

SAN FRANCISCO AND THE BAY AREA

Daytime Diversions

At Stow Lake (in the heart of Golden Gate Park), the two of you can rent a paddle boat for your own private cruise. The trail around the lake is perfect for a quiet stroll. The park's Japanese Tea Garden (near the lake and art museums) is another romantic spot. You'll follow delicate paths past a tea house, pagoda, and ponds, and over intricate bridges. The cherry blossoms bloom in spring, making the Tea Garden a special place to visit.

If you'd like to leave the crowds behind, board the Tiburon Ferry for a trip to Angel Island in San Francisco Bay. (You can even bring your bikes.) The island offers great private picnicking possibilities and enchanting city views.

Tables for Two

Julius' Castle (1541 Montgomery Street) has been rated multiple times as the city's most romantic restaurant by San Francisco Focus magazine. The view takes in both bridges and everything in between.

North Beach, the city's Italian section, is famous for intimate restaurants. One of our favorites is Fior d'Italia (601 Union Street at Stockton), San Francisco's oldest Italian restaurant. Martinelli's (Columbus at Stockton) offers cozy booths equipped with privacy curtains.

In Half Moon Bay, try Pasta Moon or San Benito House. Near Half Moon Bay overlooking the sea is Moss Beach Distillery, a former residence that serves informal dinners.

After Hours

For quiet conversation and drinks, the top floor of the Fairmont (Mason at California) boasts one of the city's finest views, made even more special by a ride up the outside glass elevator. Depending on the time of day or night, you might be riding all by yourselves. Elsewhere in the Fairmont, the Tonga is a Polynesian-themed restaurant and watering-hole complete with indoor thunderstorms.

The Compass Rose at the posh Westin St. Francis Hotel (Powell at Geary) is an elegant, romantic, old San Francisco-style lounge decorated with exquisite antiques. Some of the room's warm, cozy nooks overlook Union Square.

Archbishops Mansion Inn

1000 Fulton Street
San Francisco, CA 94117
Telephone: (415) 563-7872; toll-free: (800) 543-5820

Fifteen rooms and suites, twelve with fireplaces, three
with tubs for two. Complimentary afternoon wine
service in parlor and continental breakfast delivered
to your room in a basket. Two-night minimum stay
on weekends. Smoking is allowed. No handicapped
access. Moderate to deluxe.

Getting There
Take Fell Street exit from Highway 101 north; five
blocks west on Fell, right onto Steiner, two blocks
north to Fulton.

ARCHBISHOPS MANSION INN

San Francisco

*E*arly during a visit to the stately Archbishops Mansion, our traveling companions joked about whether a suitable romantic mood could be kindled in a dwelling that over the years had hosted a procession of priests, nuns, and high-ranking Catholic officials.

The next morning, we asked one of our friends if the inn's religious history had cooled their evening. "Not at all," he noted, shooting a knowing wink at his wife. "We would have made the archbishop blush."

Indeed, the inn's former residents and visitors would be more than a little shocked at the antics that take place behind closed doors here these days, what with cozy fireplaces, canopied beds, and the like. Other than the name, not much remains to remind visitors of the inn's interesting past.

The spartan furnishings of yesteryear (the mansion housed a succession of archbishops over a period of some forty years) have given way to a trove of beautiful objets d'art, antiques, and other pieces that include Noel Coward's grand piano and an elaborate chandelier that reportedly made an appearance in *Gone With the Wind*. Guest rooms, nicely updated while maintaining period charm, are also decorated with handsome furnishings dating back to the nineteenth century.

Rooms for Romance

We sampled Traviata, a first-floor, two-room corner suite. The sitting room held a small fireplace with mirrored mantle and several antiques, and was illuminated by several sunny windows. The bedroom, accessible only through the bathroom, was dominated by a French-carved canopied bed and elegant old armoire.

The Gypsy Baron (high $200 range) is the inn's honeymoon suite, with a large fireplace and tub for two. Double spa tubs are also found in the Der Rosenkavalier and Romeo and Juliet suites (high $100 range). In the ultimate Don Giovanni Suite (high $200 range), originally the archbishops' room, guests are treated to a large parlor, two fireplaces (one is in the bathroom), and an antique bed from a French castle. The second floor Carmen Suite (around $200) features an expansive bathroom with a clawfoot tub and its own fireplace.

While some rooms at the inn command rates in the $200 range, romantics on a budget may sample a couple of cozy rooms with canopied beds priced in the low $100 range. Three rooms with fireplaces have rates in the mid $100 range.

Don't forget to take a walk to the top of the hillside square for one of San Francisco's most often photographed views: a row of colorful Victorians over which the stunning city skyline looms.

The Majestic

1500 Sutter Street (at Gough)
San Francisco, CA 94109
Telephone: (800) 869-8966

Fifty-nine rooms and suites, each with private bath.
Many have four-poster, canopied beds, gas fireplaces,
and clawfoot soaking tubs (with shower). Valet parking provided. Amenities (in suites only) include terry
bathrobes, hairdryers, and refrigerators. Romantic
getaway packages available. Smoking is permitted.
No handicapped access. Moderate to deluxe.

Getting There
From Highway 101, take the Van Ness Avenue exit
and drive several blocks. Turn left on Pine Street and
left on Gough Street. Hotel is on the corner of Sutter
and Gough streets.

THE MAJESTIC

San Francisco

*T*hey say you'll find a city's best restaurant by asking where the locals eat. As we discovered, this is a pretty good method for locating a romantic hotel. At The Majestic, an early 1900s-vintage mansion-turned-hotel, you'll not likely run into too many tourists sporting "I ♥ San Francisco" T-shirts. According to the management, this hotel is a favorite among Bay Area folks looking for a weekend getaway in the city.

Outside, the stately Edwardian façade hasn't changed much over the years. And while the interior was all but gutted during a major renovation, the decor, from rich, hand-milled English carpeting to twinkling chandeliers, is true to the earlier era.

Although we're usually anxious to settle into our room, we poked around The Majestic's lobby area before checking in. We followed the convivial conversation in the hotel cafe, whose horseshoe-shaped bar came from an old Parisian bistro. Around the bar hangs an unusual collection of butterflies from all over the globe.

Rooms for Romance

As he turned the key to Room 403, our bellman shot us a wink. "This is my favorite room," he said. While we immediately suspected he might heap similar praise on a basement room next to the boiler, it was immediately obvious he wasn't just hankering for a big tip. Sunlight streamed through the five-window, corner bay, and a four-poster, canopied, queen-sized bed sat in the middle of the red-hued room. A gas fireplace flickered in one corner. The

bellman, who'd led many couples to this romantic hideaway before, was quickly on his way.

Although each room at The Majestic is styled differently, the layout and decor of our (grand deluxe) room was similar to that found in Rooms 203 and 303. Not being accustomed to street noise, we worried that the traffic on Gough Street might keep us awake at night. It didn't. If quiet is important, however, Room 512—facing less noisy Sutter Street— is a good choice.

The Majestic offers four accommodation types: small (low $100 range); deluxe rooms (low to mid $100 range) with fireplaces and large baths, many with clawfoot soaking tubs and double sinks; grand deluxe rooms (mid $100 range) described above; and suites (low $200 range), which offer bathrobes, refrigerators, two phones, fireplaces (visible from bed), and beautifully decorated sitting rooms.

Although The Majestic is several blocks from the downtown shopping area, we gladly surrendered the car upon arrival (the hotel provides valet parking) and found public transportation and walking to be enjoyable, functional alternatives. In the daytime, Union Square is a pleasant, invigorating walk, or a short ride away in the hotel limousine shuttle offered twice each weekday morning. At night, cab fare to the theater district was less than what it would cost to park the car.

THE MANSION HOTEL

2220 Sacramento Street
San Francisco, CA 94115
Telephone: (415) 929-9444

Twenty-one rooms and suites, each with private bathroom, some with woodburning stoves or fireplaces.
Restaurant. Magic or music concerts every night.
Amenities include bathrobes and hairdryers; a silk
rose is placed on your pillow at night. Full breakfast
included. Smoking is allowed. No handicapped
access. Moderate to deluxe.

Getting There
From Highway 101 north in San Francisco, take Van
Ness Avenue exit; follow Van Ness one mile to
Sacramento Street; turn left, four blocks to hotel.

THE MANSION HOTEL

San Francisco

$\mathcal{T}$he setting is a prim and proper mansion in San Francisco's most exclusive neighborhood. But what's this? Blazing wall murals of picnicking and pool-shooting pigs? A caged macaw and cooing doves? The saw-playing innkeeper performing in the parlor? Hardly what you'd expect to find in staid Pacific Heights.

While we foreswore applying the abused and overused word, unique, to any of the descriptions in this book, The Mansion Hotel left me no choice. It's likely the most unique overnight adventure you'll hope to experience in Northern California.

We must admit, the term garish came to mind upon stepping into the grand foyer. But after adjusting to the visual overload, we began exploring, with anticipation, the myriad parlors and hallways, wondering what on earth we'd discover next. There are whimsical objets d'art with a predominating pig theme (the innkeeper calls this "porkabilia"); millions of dollars worth of museum-quality works of art including mosaics and sculptures by Bufano; and magnificent Victorian ornaments.

Rooms for Romance

The high-spirited themes of the public rooms are carried, with gusto, into guest chambers. Among the unusual touches are walls emblazoned with murals paying tribute to folks associated with San Francisco history and lore. For example, Mrs. Charles Crocker, wife of the railroad czar, overlooks the Crocker Room, a bay-windowed, second-floor room with queen-sized bed and red carpet.

A favorite among brides (many weddings take place here) is the outlandishly styled Empress Josephine room (around $225), with Louis XIV antique furnishings, including the largest armoire I've ever seen. French doors open to a large, private, front-facing balcony, and the bath has a window that overlooks the rear garden. Entry to the opulent room is via the hotel's restaurant, up a private set of stairs.

Around back, off the garden, is the privately situated Celebrity Suite (around $200). Inside is an unusual and tasteful combination of Oriental and American antiques, queen-sized brass bed, and woodburning stove. This room has the most romantic bath, decorated in black and equipped with big spa tub and wet bar.

The hotel expanded in recent years with the acquisition of the mansion next door, an inn formerly known as the Hermitage House. A foyer now connects the two. The new addition, referred to as the West Wing, features accommodations sporting more traditional, country decor.

Among the rooms here is the front-facing, yellow and white colored Master Bedroom (high $100 range) on the second floor, equipped with a king-sized bed and a fireplace. The bathroom has a clawfoot tub into which the two of you might be able to squeeze, in a pinch.

By the way, you might consider spending a little more on your room at The Mansion Hotel. After all, just think what you'll save on San Francisco museum admission and entertainment tickets. It's all here.

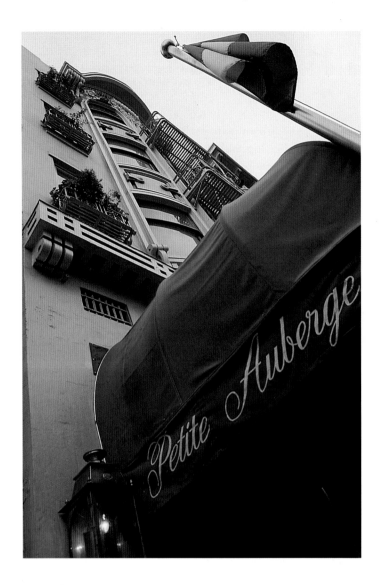

Petite Auberge

863 Bush Street
San Francisco, CA 94108
Telephone: (415) 928-6000

Twenty-six rooms, each with private bath; seventeen
with gas fireplaces. Afternoon wine and appetizers
included. Amenities include bathrobes, fresh flowers,
and morning newspaper. Full breakfast in bed available. Smoking is not permitted. No handicapped
access. Moderate to expensive.

Getting There
From Highway 101 north (Van Ness Avenue), east on
Bush to inn; inn is two and a half blocks from Union
Square.

Petite Auberge

San Francisco

*I*t took only one visit to a downtown, highrise chain hotel to convince us never to do it again. This city is just too special and our time alone too fleeting to settle for a forgettable night in some big anonymous box.

Only a stone's throw from those hulking, big names of the hotel industry, Petite Auberge, with its delicately ornate, Baroque design, and curved bay windows, has established quite a reputation among those of us who think small. What it lacks in numbers of rooms, this little French country retreat more than makes up for in charm and comfort.

Rooms for Romance

On the second floor, placed at the back of the inn, far from any traffic noise, room 26 (mid $100 range) is classified as a large room. Like the rest of the hostelry, it's done in a French country theme. This room is furnished with reproduction antiques, queen-sized bed, armoire, bookshelves, an old writing desk, and gas fireplace. The tiled bathroom holds a pedestal sink and tub-and-shower combination. Room 56 has a similar configuration, but is on the fifth floor.

A bit more compact is room 25 (medium size; low to mid $100 range), with two large windows (side-facing; no view), fireplace with carved and painted mantlepiece, and a queen-sized bed.

The charming, front-facing rooms (31, 41, and 51) feature cozy window seats in the curved bays, but they also face busy Bush Street.

Our favorite room is 10, the Petite Suite. Reached by a very private outdoor walkway off the dining-room area, the suite (low $200 range) features lace curtains, the inn's only king-sized bed, wet bar, refrigerator, fireplace, and lots of shelves with country-style knicknacks. The bathroom has a rather compact spa tub, into which both of you might be able to squeeze. French doors open to the suite's private, sunny redwood deck.

The Sherman House

2160 Green Street
San Francisco, CA 94123
Telephone: (415) 563-3600;
toll-free: (800) 424-5777

Fourteen rooms and suites; thirteen have fireplaces; two have Roman-style tubs. Restaurant. Amenities include bathrobes, hair dryers, and refrigerators. Valet parking available. Smoking is permitted. Handicapped access. Deluxe.

Getting There
From the Golden Gate Bridge, follow Highway 101 which becomes Lombard Street. Turn right on Fillmore Street and drive up the hill to Green Street. Turn left to inn on left. From northbound Highway 101, follow signs to Golden Gate Bridge and take the Fell Street exit. Drive straight up Fell for several blocks and turn right on Webster Street. After about one and a half miles, turn left on Green Street to inn on right.

SHERMAN HOUSE

San Francisco

With most rooms carrying tariffs of $350 and up (that's per night), the Sherman House is among a select few occupying San Francisco's niche of small, very exclusive luxury hotels. Generally visited by the more well-heeled or by those who've saved up to celebrate a very special occasion, the Sherman House represents the ultimate in overnight indulgence.

Built in 1876 as the home for music company founder Leander Sherman (of Sherman Clay), the mansion was considered among the city's most elegant. It served as a private residence until the mid-1980s when a new owner restored the home, carriage house, and gardens to create the hotel. A new, more customer-sensitive management team has taken the helm since our first edition.

Rooms for Romance

Most of us can only dream about savoring the top-of-the-line rooms here. Take Suite 503, for example. Located on the second floor of the restored Carriage House, the suite features a white, diamond-patterned carpet and sunken living room with French doors that open to a three-sided balcony overlooking San Francisco Bay. The one-night rate is in the mid $500 range.

For $600-plus per night you can luxuriate in the Leander Sherman Suite, the most expensive accommodation featured in this guide. Guests are treated to a sweeping view of

the Golden Gate Bridge and Alcatraz, as well as a Roman tub and fireplace.

In the low to mid $300 range are Room 201, with English furnishings and a bay view, and Room 402, which features an intimate seating alcove and Roman tub.

A series of garden rooms with queen-sized feather beds and views of the Carriage House carry rates in the $200 range.

The White Swan Inn

845 Bush Street
San Francisco, CA 94108
Telephone: (415) 755-1755

Twenty-six rooms, each with private bath and gas
fireplace. Amenities include in-room refrigerators,
morning paper, and bathrobes. Full buffet breakfast
and afternoon tea included. Smoking is not permitted.
No handicapped access. Moderate to deluxe.

Getting There
From Highway 101 (Van Ness Avenue), turn east on
Bush Street to inn. The inn is two-and-half blocks to
Union Square and one and a half blocks to Powell
Street cable car line.

THE WHITE SWAN INN

San Francisco

*M*embers of the Post family, who operate several other San Francisco inns, apparently couldn't rest until giving San Francisco visitors yet another romantic lodging alternative with their exquisite renovation of an early 1900s era hotel.

The White Swan Inn drew its inspiration from the inns of old England. The library and living rooms, with well-stocked bookshelves, flickering fireplace, and handsome English antiques in rich, warm woods will make you feel more like a tourist in London.

Rooms for Romance

Rooms at The White Swan are differentiated not so much by amenities and decor (they're all equipped with gas fireplaces, wet bars, private bathrooms, and nice furnishings), but by size.

Rooms are classified according to bed size. Room 44 (mid $100 range) on the fourth floor is a queen-bedded room with a small bathroom. It faces the side of the hotel and features a nice bay with window seat, although without a view.

While we found the queen bedroom adequate in size, the king rooms, offered for about $20 more, are larger still. We visited Room 47 which had a separate dressing area with sink.

The windows in this sunny room comprised almost an entire wall, with no view to speak of. This and the other king-bedded rooms whose numbers end with a 6 or 7 all face the back of the property and are among the most quiet.

Since our first visit, the inn has created a pair of honeymoon suites (from around $200 to the mid $200 range) with canopied beds and refrigerators stocked with complimentary gourmet chocolates.

PILLAR POINT INN

380 Capistrano Road
Princeton-by-the-Sea, CA
Mailing address: P.O. Box 388, El Granada, CA 94018
Telephone: (415) 728-7377

Eleven rooms, all with ocean/harbor views, private baths,
fireplaces, VCRs, refrigerators, and feather beds. Full
gourmet breakfast and complimentary food items included.
Smoking is not permitted. Handicapped access. Moderate
to expensive.

Getting There
From Highway 1, four miles north of Half Moon Bay, drive
west (toward ocean) into the harbor area at Capistrano
Road to inn.

PILLAR POINT INN

Princeton-by-the-Sea

*W*e had traveled the scenic Highway 1 route between Santa Cruz and San Francisco dozens of times, but it wasn't until Pillar Point Inn opened that we realized there was such a place as Princeton-by-the-Sea.

If you're seeking a destination resort or city, this sleepy community won't rank high on the list. However, as a cozy stopover or an alternative romantic getaway spot that's quickly accessible (less than one hour) from most anywhere in the Bay Area, Pillar Point Inn fits the bill.

The contemporary, New England-styled hostelry overlooks bustling Pillar Point Harbor on the ocean side of the San Francisco peninsula, just a few miles north of Half Moon Bay.

When creating the establishment just a few years ago, Pillar Point's builders could easily have followed the California hotel crowd and aimed for quantity. Instead, they chose not to ruin a good thing and the inn's size was held to only a few cozy rooms.

Rooms for Romance

With less than a dozen guestrooms to furnish, the inn could afford to splurge. Each room is equipped with antique reproductions (down to the radios and refrigerators), VCRs, tiled fireplaces, and brass and porcelain feather beds. All but one have window seats that overlook the harbor.

Although ground-level rooms feature enclosed tubs that convert to steam baths, a second-floor room offers a bit more distance from busy Capistrano Road that runs in front of the inn. (Double-paned windows do keep the traffic noise down, but passing cars can be heard when windows are open to take advantage of ocean breezes.)

Decor doesn't vary much from room-to-room, but Rooms 6 and 10, both second-floor end units, have Palladian-style arched windows and a touch more privacy (neighbors on only one side). Room 10 is slightly bigger and contains a king-sized bed.

Cypress Inn on Miramar Beach

407 Mirada Road
Half Moon Bay, CA 94019
Telephone: (415) 726-6002;
toll-free in California: (800) 83BEACH

Twelve rooms, each with private bath, fireplace, and ocean-view deck. Full breakfast and afternoon tea included. Amenities include comforters, down pillows, and bottled water in your room. Smoking is not permitted. Handicapped access. Expensive to deluxe.

Getting There
From Highway 1, twenty-six miles south of San Francisco, turn west onto Medio Avenue and follow to inn on the corner of Medio and Mirada.

CYPRESS INN ON MIRAMAR BEACH

Half Moon Bay

*F*or the folks who run Cypress Inn on Miramar Beach, a beautiful but off-the-beaten-track location is a mixed blessing. Although they don't get too many drive-bys, guests who have discovered this contemporary hideaway enjoy not only solitude but quick access (a dozen steps) to a five-mile stretch of white sandy beach.

Mexican folk art is the unusual theme here, and it's carried through from food to furnishings. When we dropped in one afternoon, the staff had just assembled a midday snack of chips, salsa, and other spicy treats in the dining area on the ground floor. (The complimentary full breakfast, however, includes more north-of-the-border fare such as peaches and cream French toast, omelets, and waffles.)

Rooms for Romance

El Sol, a sunny, lower-level corner room, is painted a bold yellow and decorated with wooden pillars, a tiled fireplace, and live cacti. On the second floor, El Viento beckons with a warm, pink theme.

Las Nubes, the third-floor penthouse suite, is the inn's largest and most romantic room, featuring magnificent ocean views, large private deck, a cushy sofa near the fireplace, and spa tub for two. Per-night tariff for Las Nubes is in the high $200 range. One room is offered in the $150 range, although most carry rates in the mid to high $100 range.

Each room features terra-cotta tile floors (with radiant heat), a comforter, down pillows, a fireplace, a writing desk, and a small sundeck. All have ocean views.

East Brother Light Station

117 Park Place
Point Richmond, CA 94801
Telephone: (510) 233-2385

Four rooms, one with shower/tub. Dinner and break-
fast included. Open Thursday through Sunday.
Smoking is not permitted. No handicapped access.
Deluxe.

Getting There
Guests are ferried to the island from Point San Pablo
Yacht Harbor on the Richmond side of the bay in
Contra Costa County. The innkeepers will send a
map with confirmation.

EAST BROTHER LIGHT STATION

Point Richmond

"*G*etting away from it all" takes on a whole new meaning when you're sleeping on a one-acre island a quarter-mile out in San Francisco Bay. Except for (no more than) three other couples, the innkeeper, and resident gulls, it's just the two of you.

One of the oldest establishments listed in our guide, East Brother Light Station was built in 1873 and is the oldest of all the West Coast lighthouses still in operation. That's right. The old beacon still sweeps the bay and the fog horn still blows from October through March. Guests can even wander up the tower stairs for a close look at the powerful working lens.

The light station was tended by keepers for much of its history, but the facilities went downhill after the Coast Guard automated the signals in 1969. A decade later, a nonprofit group was organized to restore and preserve the station for public use, and overnight visitors soon followed.

Since you can't come and go at will, guests are treated to dinner as well as a hot breakfast. At the time of our travels, cost per couple, per night was around $300, including food.

It's important to note that only one room, the Marin, has a shower/bathtub, and it can only be used if you're visiting for more than one night. Water, which is collected in a cistern from winter rains, is usually in short supply. Basins, however, are provided in two rooms.

Rooms for Romance

The Marin Room is on the second floor and—like the other three rooms here—is decorated with antique furniture and Laura Ashley fabrics. On a clear day, Mount Tamalpais and the Marin County coast are visible from your queen-sized brass bed. This is the room most favored by visiting honeymoon couples.

The San Francisco Room, so-named for the glorious view of the city afforded from its windows, is furnished in similar decor, also with a queen-sized bed. The small bath in this room does not have bathtub/shower facilities. Be advised that the downstairs rooms share a bathroom with tub and shower.

If the solitude of your lighthouse room gets to be too overwhelming, there's always dinner, when the other guests (if there are any) gather in the dining room for the innkeepers' sumptuous, four-course meal, complete with wine and candlelight.

A final note: Make sure you eat your fill at dinner. If you get a craving for a Big Mac later on, it's a long swim.

CASA MADRONA HOTEL

801 Bridgeway
Sausalito, CA 94965
Telephone: (415) 332-0502

Thirty-four rooms and suites, each with private bath;
sixteen have fireplaces and four have tubs for two.
Highly rated restaurant. Amenities include outdoor
spa, valet parking, bubblebath, bathrobes, refrigerators, and blow dryers. Continental breakfast and daily
social hour included. Smoking is allowed.
Handicapped access. Moderate to deluxe.

Getting There
From Highway 101 north, exit at Alexander Avenue,
to Bridgeway. From Highway 101 south, take
Marin/Sausalito exit to Bridgeway.

Casa Madrona Hotel

Sausalito

*C*hoosing a romantic room at Casa Madrona is like making a selection from the menu of a four-star restaurant. It'll make you hungry, but you'll definitely have trouble deciding. To make it a tiny bit easier, the good folks here have added little asterisks to the room menu alongside the names of ten rooms "particularly suited for honeymoons or other special occasions." They know what we're looking for.

This enchanting hotel is draped over a green, Sausalito hillside overlooking San Francisco Bay, and most of the rooms are situated to take full advantage of this inspiring setting.

Rooms for Romance

At the top of the hill is the Victorian House, a stately old mansion which for many years comprised the entire inn. (The new wing was added only a few years ago.) Among the dozen rooms in the manor house is La Salle (low $100 range; garden view), decorated in French country and complemented by a dual spa tub. The Belle Vista Suite (high $100 range) offers a romantic San Francisco skyline view and a freestanding tub for two in the living room.

The gabled and balconied rooms of the New Casa sweep artfully down the hillside below the manor house. Rooms here are modern, and come in many shapes, sizes, and styles. In the mid $100 range is Kathmandu, where huge cushions encourage lounging and tiny nooks invite exploring. A fireplace and tub for two complete this room.

Also worth noting are the Rose Chalet (pine furniture, separate bed alcove, fireplace, deck, and view) and the Renoir Room, where guests luxuriate in a clawfoot tub surrounded by a garden mural. There's also a window seat, fireplace, and deck from which to enjoy a spectacular bay view.

Three cottages complete the Casa Madrona complex. La Tonnelle, for example, is offered at around $165, and features a woodburning stove, king-sized bed, bay view, and private patio. The hotel describes this retreat as the greatest hideout in Sausalito.

THE CENTRAL COAST

Daytime Diversions

While everyone has their sights set on the shops of Carmel, too many folks miss the chance to stroll the beautiful, white-sand beach along Carmel Bay. Don't miss it, especially on a sunny day. The beach is only a short walk from the heart of the village.

In Monterey, Northern California's other Fisherman's Wharf is crammed with little, open-air markets that display a variety of fresh catches. Monterey also has a historic section where many buildings, some dating back to the Spanish and Mexican eras, are open for uncrowded exploring. (These are within walking distance of the Old Monterey Inn.)

There's a paved pedestrian and bike path along the bay between Cannery Row and Pacific Grove. Surrey rentals are available along the path. Despite the foot and cycle traffic, it's one of the most romantic promenades you'll ever take.

Tables for Two

For a fun, convivial atmosphere, drop by the Rio Grill (California cuisine) in the Crossroads Center off Highway 1 just south of Carmel on Rio Road. Another recommended spot is Fandango's (continental and Basque), 223 Seventeenth Street in Pacific Grove.

Among gourmets, the highest marks go to Fresh Cream, a critically acclaimed French restaurant in Monterey's Heritage Harbor near Fisherman's Wharf. Another good choice for French fare is Melacs at 663 Lighthouse Avenue in Pacific Grove. Gernot's, 649 Lighthouse Avenue, was recommended by more than one of our innkeeping hosts.

Ventana's highly rated on-site restaurant (early reservations advised) is accessible to resort guests via a winding, romantic path through the Big Sur forest. Trail-side lights will guide you and other hand-holding couples back to your rooms after dinner.

After Hours

In Carmel village, stop for a warm drink at the Hog's Breath Inn (San Carlos and Fifth Avenue), which has been operated for many years by actor and former Carmel mayor Clint Eastwood. The evening chill of the intimate courtyard seating area is tempered by outdoor heaters.

OLD MONTEREY INN

500 Martin Street
Monterey, CA 93940
Telephone: (408) 375-8284

Ten rooms and suites, eight with fireplaces. Amenities include in-room refrigerators with complimentary drinks, bathrobes, extra towels, hair dryers, and grooming items. Full breakfast served. Afternoon wine/tea hour with homemade goodies. Adults only. Smoking is not permitted. No handicapped access. Expensive to deluxe.

Getting There
Monterey is one hundred fifteen miles south of San Francisco on Highway 1. From Pacific Street near the city's historic section, head east on Martin. The inn is situated in a residential area and is marked by a small sign on the right side of Martin Street.

OLD MONTEREY INN

Monterey

*W*e had a hunch we were in for a treat after the second or third pass along Martin Street searching for Old Monterey Inn. In our experience, the harder an inn is to find, the more special it is.

Our theory was confirmed when we finally spotted the inn's tiny sign in a tree and entered the wooded property of Gene and Ann Swett, proprietors of what one publication termed one of the most romantic hideaways in the world.

After a short time with Ann, it became obvious why innkeepers and prospective innkeepers from far and wide drop by Old Monterey Inn to learn a thing or two about the business. The level of service and accommodations here would rival most any inn or hotel we've visited. The Swetts have gone the extra mile, and it shows.

The Tudor-style, craftsman estate in which the Swetts raised six children contains ten guest rooms, each with private bath and each offering a different guest experience, thanks to Ann's decorating flourishes. Gene, the resident green thumb, is responsible for the English-style gardens that are in constant color.

Rooms for Romance

Seven rooms are under the roof of the main house. Among these is The Library (high $100 range), a second-floor room with king-sized bed, stone fireplace, and a small, private sundeck. The peaceful view of trees and gardens complements the cozy decor Ann has created, with rows of bookshelves generously stocked with intriguing titles. This spot would make the dreariest Monterey Bay day pleasant.

One of the main house's most private hideaways is Dovecote, the rear-facing, third-floor room decorated in what Ann calls a hunting theme. A fireplace, king-sized bed, window seat, and skylight are among the thoughtful features here.

We were particularly intrigued by Serengeti, a Carriage House room inspired by Ann's vision of a turn-of-the-century African safari. That's right! If you've ever wondered what it's like sleeping under a genuine jungle mosquito net, save the airfare. It's all here, including an authentic safari hat, vintage camera, antique field glasses, and a spa tub for two. A sweet-smelling stash of potpourri sat in an old cigar box. This room is offered in the $200 range.

Our home for the night was the Garden Cottage (low $200 range), a spacious suite with cozy sitting room, fireplace, and step-up bedroom. The shuttered windows filtered an elevated view through limbs of twisting oaks into the garden beyond. Skylights illuminated the entire suite.

Rooms at Old Monterey Inn are well-stocked, not only with complimentary beverages, but with toothpaste and even shaving accessories. Two designer bathrobes hang in the closet. Many rooms have luxurious feather beds.

Depending on your mood (or the unpredictable Monterey weather), complimentary full breakfast is served either in the impressive dining room, outdoors in the garden, or in your room. Although we'd planned to dine under our warm, down comforter, the morning sun drew us into the garden with several other guests for a memorable breakfast of waffles, whipped cream, and berries.

Spindrift Inn

652 Cannery Row
Monterey, CA 93940
Telephone: (408) 646-8900;
toll-free: (800) 841-1879

Forty-one rooms, all with woodburning fireplaces.
Half of the rooms have bay views or balconies.
Amenities include bathrobes, bubblebath, and an
afternoon wine/tea social. Noon checkout time.
Continental breakfast and morning newspaper delivered to your room. Smoking is allowed. Handicapped
access. Expensive to deluxe.

Getting There
From Highway 101 in Monterey, take Del Monte
Avenue exit and drive through town. Follow signs to
Cannery Row. The inn is at the heart of Cannery
Row on the bay side of the street.

SPINDRIFT INN

Monterey

For those expecting to experience John Steinbeck's Cannery Row, a trip down the narrow Row during a busy weekend can be a disheartening experience. Tour buses hog the parking lots, tourists clog the streets, and many of the original buildings have been replaced by stucco façades.

At night, however, the picture changes completely. When the cars and tourists leave, the fog sometimes settles in, bringing with it the smells and sounds of the Cannery Row described by Steinbeck. In the early morning, lapping waves and a distant foghorn are all that can be heard. Nights and mornings offer an enchanting taste of what the fabled street must have been like before the tourists came.

Despite its modernization, Cannery Row is still a magical lovers' getaway, especially when savored from the Spindrift Inn. Built on the beach on the site of an old cannery, the inn offers considerable serenity despite its location at the heart of the Row.

Rooms for Romance

Although our room faced Cannery Row, we could also see the bay thanks to an expansive set of corner windows. With the exception of views, rooms here are similar. Furnishings include fireplaces, canopied and draped feather beds, and comforters. The marble baths feature brass fixtures and a second telephone. Remote-controlled televisions are hidden in armoires.

The inn is just down the street from the Monterey Bay Aquarium and a short jaunt from Fisherman's Wharf. A bike/walking path hugs the coastline connecting the Row with quaint Pacific Grove and the wharf.

At the time of our last visit, the inn was offering a romantic retreat dinner package on certain days.

Gosby House Inn

643 Lighthouse Avenue
Pacific Grove, CA 93950
Telephone: (408) 375-1287

Twenty-two rooms, some facing downtown; others
facing an interior garden area. Twelve rooms have fireplaces; all but two rooms have private baths, two with
antique clawfoot tubs. Amenities include full breakfast
(available in bed), turn-down service, morning paper,
bathrobes, afternoon hors d'oeuvres and wine, and
bicycles. Smoking is not permitted. Handicapped
access. Moderate to expensive.

Getting There
From Highway 1, take Highway 68 west to Pacific
Grove. Highway 68 becomes Forest Avenue; continue
on Forest; turn left on Lighthouse Avenue, three
blocks to the inn.

GOSBY HOUSE INN

Pacific Grove

*I*n our search for peace and quiet, we usually shun hostelries situated at the heart of a town. An exception is Gosby House Inn. Although its location can be described as downtown, this isn't your typical town. Pacific Grove is sleepy compared to its bustling neighbors, Monterey and Carmel. The few businesses along Lighthouse Avenue cater largely to the townsfolk, many of whom reside in tidy Victorians built a hundred years ago.

A Pacific Grove landmark, Gosby House is among the stately structures that have been around since the community's founding as a religious and educational retreat center. In fact, J. F. Gosby, the inn's namesake, opened the Queen Anne-style structure to Pacific Grove's early visitors back in the 1880s.

All but two of the Gosby's rooms have private baths. Twelve have fireplaces, and most have queen-sized beds. (A handful of rooms have double beds. Make sure to specify a queen room if you desire one.) A full breakfast can be taken with other guests in the parlor of the main house or brought to your room.

Rooms for Romance

It may appear relatively small from the street, but the Gosby House holds twenty-two rooms. Ours, called the William LaPorte Suite, was among those added on as Mr. Gosby's

business blossomed. Attached to, but set behind the main house, the cottage-style room features country decor, a fireplace, and a sunny, private patio situated off the main path. Carriage House rooms have recently been upgraded with spa tubs.

Four of the inn's most romantic rooms—all with queen beds and fireplaces—are situated upstairs in the main house. Their names are Harrison McKinley, Robert Louis Stevenson, Holman, and Gosby. All are offered in the mid $100 range.

Lovers Point (low $100 range) also has an outside entry with private patio, as well as a fireplace that can be savored from the queen-sized bed.

For lovers on a budget, Gosby House Inn is a bargain. Although you won't pay ocean-view prices (many rooms were in the $100 range at the time of our visit), the coast is only a short stroll away.

Green Gables Inn

104 Fifth Street
Pacific Grove, CA 93950
Telephone: (408) 375-2095

Eleven rooms, six with private baths; six with fireplaces. Breakfast (served buffet-style) with hot entree
and evening appetizers/wine included. Smoking is not
permitted. No handicapped access. Moderate to
expensive.

Getting There
From Highway 1, take Highway 68 west to Pacific
Grove. Highway 68 becomes Forest Avenue; continue
on Forest Avenue; at the beach, turn right on Ocean
View Boulevard to inn, corner of Fifth Street.

GREEN GABLES INN

Pacific Grove

hey don't make 'em like they used to." We don't know who coined the phrase, but he or she must have been describing this sublime place. An architectural show-stopper in its own right, the Green Gables Inn is doubly spectacular given its locale. If the water were any closer, you could fish from your window.

Only a two-lane road separates this lovely half-timbered Victorian from Monterey Bay, and most of the distinctive gabled rooms have dramatic views of the sea or coastline.

Rooms for Romance

Among returning guests, the most often asked-for room (even though it shares a bath) is Balcony (low $100 range), on the second floor. One of the particularly appealing attractions of this room, in addition to the ocean view, is the step-down sun porch with daybed. There's no need to draw the drapes for privacy since neither the adjacent street nor bike path is visible from your bed. Just enjoy the spectacular view.

Another popular room, Chapel (low $100 range), features old mahogany, an open-beam ceiling, and step-up window seat. It shares a pair of easily accessible bathrooms with three other rooms.

Jennifer's Room, which does have its own bath with shower, has a huge wall-length window and a brass and iron bed.

The huge Lacey Suite is the inn's most expensive accommodation, priced in the mid $100 range. It holds a queen-sized bed, a private bath with antique tub, a huge armoire that covers almost an entire wall, and a sitting room with a gas fireplace. The sitting room and bedchamber are separated by a pretty sliding door. The suite does not have an ocean view and is located directly off the living room.

Elsewhere in the main house is Garrett, which we found a bit too small. It also shares a bath.

While the fairy-tale façade of the main house can prove hard to resist, many guests head for the separate three-level Carriage House whose rooms (mid $100 range) all have partial ocean views, king-sized beds, gas fireplaces, and private baths. These rooms are spacious but lack the antique charm of the main house.

Whichever room you choose, you'll be greeted by two teddy bears placed somewhere in your chambers.

SEVEN GABLES INN

555 Ocean View Boulevard
Pacific Grove, CA 93950
Telephone: (408) 372-4341

Fourteen rooms, each with private bath and expansive
bay/ocean/coastal view. Continental breakfast and
afternoon high tea included. Two-night minimum
stay on weekends. Romance package available.
Smoking is not permitted. Handicapped access.
Moderate to deluxe.

Getting There
From Highway 1, take Pacific Grove/Pebble Beach
exit and follow signs to Pacific Grove. Road becomes
Forest Avenue; stay on Forest Avenue; turn right at
Ocean View Boulevard for two blocks to inn.

Seven Gables Inn

Pacific Grove

*A*rguably California's most beautiful Victorian inn, Seven Gables is the place you've always fantasized about. Relaxing in the front yard on a sunny afternoon, we watched car after car slow to gawking speed as they edged along Ocean View Boulevard past this classic beauty. Even though we were only there for a night, I felt like the guy at the prom with the prettiest girl.

Thanks to the resident Flatley family, those gingerbread-laden, gabled rooms that for years could only be enjoyed from street level can now be savored from the inside. It's true that the stately exterior sets lofty expectations. But the interior is up to the task. The public rooms that greet arriving guests are ostentatious displays of Victoriana, with gilded fixtures, museum-quality antiques, and ornately patterned rugs.

The period theme is carried into the guestrooms, which boast appointments like down-filled couches, inlaid tables and sideboards, antique prints, nine-foot-high armoires, and velvet-covered chairs.

Views from many of the inn's rooms are postcard-quality. Although you'll rue the setting of the sun for stealing this scene, the night kicks the other senses into high gear. The smell of the sea and sounds of crashing surf in the darkness lulled us for hours.

Rooms for Romance

Half of the fourteen rooms are located in the main house. The most coveted is Bellevue, a second-floor room with a sunny, eastern exposure and spectacular bay view framed by a windowed seating area. The Fairmont, also in the main house, looks out along the coastal boulevard toward Cannery Row. Rates for both are in the mid $100 range.

A cozy guest house and cottage complete the Seven Gables' list of accommodations. In the guest house, our favorite room is the Cypress (low $200 range), where a corner bay window affords an unforgettable, 180-degree view of the bay. Other touches include a pressed tin ceiling and stained-glass windows.

A floor-to-ceiling Tiffany window adorns the Victoria Room (mid $100 range), also in the guest house. The room is accented with velvet furnishings and canopied bed. The view from here is also impressive.

Breakfast at Seven Gables, which includes a hot entree, is a convivial, sit-down affair in the inn's ornate dining room.

COBBLESTONE INN

Junipero between Seventh and Eighth
(P.O. Box 3185), Carmel, CA 93921
Telephone: (408) 625-5222

Twenty-four rooms, each with private bath and gas
fireplace. Bathrobes and morning paper provided.
Breakfast buffet and afternoon wine and appetizers
included. Romance package available. Smoking is not
permitted. Handicapped access. Moderate to expensive.

Getting There
From Highway 1 at Carmel, take Ocean Avenue exit;
turn left on Junipero, two blocks to inn.

COBBLESTONE INN

Carmel

Owned by the same clan of hoteliers that operates the Gosby House and Green Gables Inns (as well as San Francisco's Petite Auberge and White Swan Inn), the Cobblestone has the same romantic charm that characterizes the other Post family establishments.

Once upon a time, this was just another plain-jane motel. But with the addition of a distinctive façade of stone from the Carmel River, a fresh, new country decor, and other bits of "Carmelization," the Cobblestone has become one of the village's most romantic retreats.

Rooms for Romance

The inn's designated honeymoon suite is Room 27, a particularly sunny hideaway (mid to high $100 range) featuring a four-poster king-sized bed and recessed sitting area under the windows. The bath has a shower/tub combination. Guests staying in this room only are treated to breakfast in bed.

Room 26 is another bright room, decked out in the inn's pervasive Laura Ashley country-style theme. But this one is priced more moderately, in the low $100 range. One of the innkeeper's personal favorites is Room 18, a sunny corner room with a pleasant local view and sitting area with sofa.

The rooms, all equipped with refrigerators and gas fireplaces, are arranged in a horseshoe shape around a well-tended, slate courtyard dotted with flower planters and small tables. The inn is set in a neighborhood with a mix of homes and businesses, and is only two blocks from the heart of Carmel village. A walk of about eight blocks will bring you to Carmel's glorious, white-sand beach.

Ventana

Big Sur, CA 93920

Telephone: (408) 667-2331; or toll-free: (800) 628-6500

Fifty-nine rooms and suites, each with private bath, refrigerator, and videocassette player. Most have fireplaces; eleven
have private outdoor spas; a few rooms have kitchens.
Amenities include bathrobes, complimentary breakfast (in
your room, if desired), and complimentary afternoon wine-
cheese bar. Mobil four-star-rated restaurant, pools, sauna,
Japanese-style baths, and on-site store. Two-night minimum
stay on weekends; three-night minimum during holidays.
Smoking is allowed. Handicapped access. Expensive to deluxe.

Getting There

Ventana is 28 miles south of the last traffic light in Carmel just
off coastal Highway 1.

VENTANA

Big Sur

Granted, the sight and sound of surf breaking just outside your window is pretty special, especially to big-city folk. But there's nothing like a fifty-mile, tree-and-sea view from high above the ocean to test one's sensual limits.

Encouraged by a couple of friends who termed Ventana a "hedonistic hideaway," we booked a room to celebrate a special birthday. Until that time, our encounters with Big Sur were primarily on four wheels as we savored the coastal beauty along Highway 1. As pleasant as those visits were, one can't fully appreciate this region without sampling Ventana. The inn is as spectacular as its setting.

Ventana's fifty-nine guest rooms are spread among some two hundred forty acres in a dozen single- and two-story units of weathered cedar. Accommodations are connected by foot paths that wind through a mountain meadow ringed by redwood, oak, and bay laurel trees. Another foot path, romantically lit at night, leads through the forest to the Ventana restaurant a short stroll away.

Rooms for Romance

Our room, # 53, The Cottage, was situated at the rear of Ventana's property, overlooking seemingly endless miles of forest. We spent much of our time relaxing in our private deck-mounted spa under the highest reaches of a grand oak.

Don't be disappointed that the management won't guarantee a specific room. You really can't go wrong with any of the accommodations here. The most seductive, found in one of the resort's more recent additions, have tiled decks with private hot tubs on the outside and fireplaces inside. Every room has either a balcony or patio, and most have ocean vistas.

Rooms are paneled with wood and are decorated in pastel blue, pink, and gold. Curtained beds with hand-painted headboards and hand-made quilts are featured throughout the inn. Accommodations vary from the not-so-standard guest room (starting in the high $100 range) to spacious fireplace/spa suites (from the mid $400 range), with lots to choose from in between.

If an expensive suite is out of reach, you'll still have access to communal Japanese-style hot baths, swimming pool, sauna, and sun deck. Clothing optional areas are also provided.

Because of the privacy-sensitive layout of the complex (not to mention the indoor enter-

tainment options), you'll likely feel alone at Ventana, even though the inn is often booked solid. The largest gathering of guests is often found in the late afternoon, sampling a sumptuous, complimentry wine-and-cheese buffet on the terrace. Continental breakfast is also served communally, but most prefer to dine in bed.

Although check-in isn't until 4:30 p.m., Ventana's 1:00 p.m. check-out time is the most generous of all our destinations.

THE MOTHER LODE, SIERRA, AND SACRAMENTO

Daytime Diversions

In the Mother Lode, grab a map and find your way along the twisting back roads to places like Daffodil Hill (about three miles north of Volcano; over three hundred thousand daffodils blooming from mid-March through mid-April) and Fiddletown, east of Plymouth.

A Gold Country visit won't be complete without a visit to a few of the region's many small wineries. The Shenandoah Valley is home to many and maps are available from the Amador County Chamber of Commerce in Jackson.

In Yosemite, grab a couple of deli sandwiches in the village and rent bicycles at Yosemite Lodge. Pedal along the many paths to a private spot in a meadow for a lunch with a view you'll never forget. The only better vistas (in our opinion) are Glacier Point above Yosemite Valley.

Visitors to Sacramento will enjoy the State Railroad Museum and a stroll along the wooden sidewalks of Old Sacramento. (Horse and buggy rides are also available.)

Tables for Two/After Hours

At dinner time in Yosemite Valley, the grand dining room in the Ahwahnee is lit with tall, slim tapers placed on each table. Music from a grand piano fills the hall. After dinner, retreat to one of the hotel's cozy public halls for quiet conversation and a warm drink. There's often an outdoor ice rink (with skate rentals) at Camp Curry during the winter. It's pure bliss under a starlit sky.

In the Gold Country our innkeepers recommend the Imperial Hotel and Ballads, both on Highway 49 in Amador City; Pelargonium (51 Hanford Street) in Sutter Creek; and Ruby Tuesday on the Eureka Street Courtyard, also in Sutter Creek. In Nevada City, we were guided to Peter Selaya's on Broad Street and Country Rose on Commercial Street, where a small creek runs through the dining patio.

In Sacramento, Harlow's Bar and Cafe (on J Street near Interstate 80) is a choice spot for an intimate dinner. Caffe Donatello (Town and Country Shopping Center) is a colorful, convivial Italian restaurant with excellent food and great atmosphere.

The Foxes in Sutter Creek

77 Main Street (P.O. Box 159)
Sutter Creek, CA 95685
Telephone: (209) 267-5882

Six rooms and suites, each with private bath.
Amenities include television tucked discreetly inside
armoires and air conditioning. Complimentary full
breakfast cooked to order and delivered to your room
with silver service. Two-night minimum on weekends.
Smoking is not permitted. No handicapped access.
Moderate.

Getting There
Sutter Creek is located on Highway 49, just north of
the Highway 88 junction, east of Lodi. The inn is
located on Highway 49, Sutter Creek's main street.

THE FOXES IN SUTTER CREEK

Sutter Creek

*B*uilt in 1857 during California's Gold Rush, this handsome, old homestead takes its name from current owners, Pete and Min Fox, the kind of folks who exemplify Sutter Creek's well-deserved moniker, "nicest town in the Mother Lode."

Unlike some of the region's bed and breakfasts, where several guests share a couple of bathrooms, the Foxes host Gold Country visitors in a half-dozen comfortable, well-equipped, nicely decorated rooms, each retrofitted with its own bath. Rooms are offered in the low $100 range.

Rooms for Romance

The Honeymoon Suite is among the inn's plushest love nests. It's a spacious room and contains a sitting area with fireplace, canopied queen-sized bed, old-fashioned tub and separate shower, period furniture, and two blue velvet wing chairs. Entry is private, from the porch overlooking the inn's garden.

The upstairs Garden Room, which overlooks the treetops, is decorated in shades of peach, teal, and cream. Two soft, pale aqua-colored velvet chairs sit before a woodburning fireplace. The queen-sized bed is partly canopied and side-draped, covered with a hand-crocheted spread.

Soft grays and blues complement the spacious upstairs Blue Room that features a balcony and private entry. Furnishings include an old-fashioned bathtub and separate shower, and a pair of dark burgundy leather wing chairs, as well as antiques.

The Foxes is centrally located in the quaint downtown area of Sutter Creek; shops and restaurants are within easy walking distance.

Gold Quartz Inn

15 Bryson Drive
Sutter Creek, CA 95685
Telephone: (209) 267-9155

Twenty-four rooms, each with private bath; twenty
with private porches. Included are full breakfast and
high tea with desserts, appetizers, and other goodies.
Smoking is not permitted. Handicapped access.
Moderate.

Getting There
Sutter Creek is located on Highway 49, east of Lodi,
just north of the Highway 88 junction. From
Highway 88, turn left onto Highway 49, follow to
Bryson Drive, and turn right.

GOLD QUARTZ INN

Sutter Creek

*E*arning three separate entries in our romantic guide to California, the Gold rush-era burg of Sutter Creek made an obvious impression. We can't imagine any couple driving through this quaint village without stopping for awhile to admire the graceful, old buildings or visit some of the boutique-style shops that dot Highway 49 downtown. And if you had the foresight to plan an overnighter, there are several cozy alternatives.

Gold Quartz Inn is among the newest, although its Victorian appearance might suggest otherwise. Built only a few years ago, the inn was given a Queen Anne design, typical of many of the town's old buildings and homes. Rooms are bright and spacious, and all have private baths and gas fireplaces. Rates here range from under $100 to the low $100 range.

Rooms for Romance

Except for some individual styling, Rooms 101 and 201 are similarly laid out. Billed as honeymoon suites, each features a carved, four-poster, step-up, king-sized bed. They also contain clawfoot tubs, separate showers, lace curtains, and private porches.

In the same price range is Room 206, one of the inn's most popular. Features include a

king-sized bed with brass headboard, sitting area with two velvet-covered chairs, lace curtains, and private porch.

Visitors should be aware that Gold Quartz Inn is located just south of downtown Sutter Creek. Consequently, you'll not be able to walk to Sutter Creek shops.

SUTTER CREEK INN

75 Main Street (P.O. Box 385)
Sutter Creek, CA 95685
Telephone: (209) 267-5606

Nineteen rooms, each with private bath and air conditioning; nine with fireplaces. Breakfast with hot entree included. Smoking is allowed in some rooms. No handicapped access. Moderate.

Getting There
From Highway 99 near Lodi, take Highway 88 to Highway 49; left to Sutter Creek; inn is located in town.

SUTTER CREEK INN

*J*ane Way, Sutter Creek Inn's longtime proprietress, is a legend among California's bed-and-breakfast innkeepers. When Jane bought the old, Greek revival-style home and opened it to guests more than twenty-five years ago, she created the West's first bed and breakfast. Although the industry has since exploded with competition, Jane and her inn continue to attract a loyal following.

With nineteen guest accommodations (all with their own bathrooms), this is among Northern California's largest bed-and-breakfast inns. Rooms are located both in the main house and in private outbuildings.

Sutter Creek Inn does feature a helping of the antique decor that characterizes the typical bed and breakfast. Jane has sprinkled the rooms with enough of her high-spirited personality to make this place memorable.

Rooms for Romance

Since our last visit, three rooms, the Library, Lower Wash House, and Tool Shed, have been redecorated in pastel colors. Each has a patio.

A favorite room is the Carriage House, with the unusual feature of his-and-her-bathrooms. It also has a canopied, queen-sized bed, sitting area, and fireplace. The weekend rate is in the low $100 range.

Porch swings overlooking the garden have earned David's Room favored status among

returning guests. This elegantly handsome room (offered for less than $100) also has a queen-sized bed, comfortable couch, and fireplace.

More feminine in decor, the West Room (less than $100) in the main house holds a large clawfoot tub (you can both squeeze in), along with a double bed and pleasant view of the garden.

The Hideaway Room contains one of Jane Way's famous swinging beds. But don't worry about being swung into space by creating too much, uh, motion. The bed can be stabilized.

Grandmere's Bed-and-Breakfast Inn

449 Broad Street
Nevada City, CA 95959
Telephone: (916) 265-4660

Seven rooms, each with private bath. Three rooms have tubs big enough for two. Vegetarian breakfast with hot entree included. Two-night minimum stay required on weekends and holidays. Smoking is not permitted. No handicapped access. Moderate to expensive.

Getting There
From Interstate 80 in Auburn, exit at Highway 49 and drive about forty-five minutes, following signs to Grass Valley. Drive past Grass Valley and exit highway at Broad Street. Turn left and follow to the top of the hill to inn on left.

GRANDMERE'S BED-
AND-BREAKFAST INN

Nevada City

*L*ocated on one of historic Nevada City's narrow streets, this three-story colonial revival mansion was once the home of Aaron Sargent who played a major part in the construction of the transcontinental railroad, and his wife, Ellen, who championed women's rights with Susan B. Anthony in the 1860s. Anthony was a frequent guest in the home.

The inn reflects its historic past, from the carriage house beside terraced and closely manicured gardens, to the creaky floors and stubborn front door lock. Blond hardwood floors brighten the sitting room where a sunny window seat and antique furnishings invite guests to curl up with a newspaper and nibble chocolates from a bottomless jar.

A number of such touches hint at the hospitality of innkeepers Doug and Geri Boka. Guests may help themselves to glassware, sodas, magazines, and umbrellas. Spicy tea and three flavors of freshly ground coffee are offered each morning before a hot, meatless breakfast, taken at a communal table or via tray to the garden or your bedroom.

Rooms for Romance

A two-room suite with a private porch entry, the Master Suite (mid $100 range) is the only room with a fireplace, which is surrounded by a sitting area. Oak steps rise to a four-poster, queen-sized bed covered with a white eyelet comforter. Knotty pine paneling encloses the private bath where a clawfoot tub seats two. A private deck furnished with white wicker chairs overlooks the garden.

Gertie's Room (mid $100 range) has a private garden entrance as well as a kitchen, a sitting area, a queen-sized, four-poster bed, and a private bath with a tub for two.

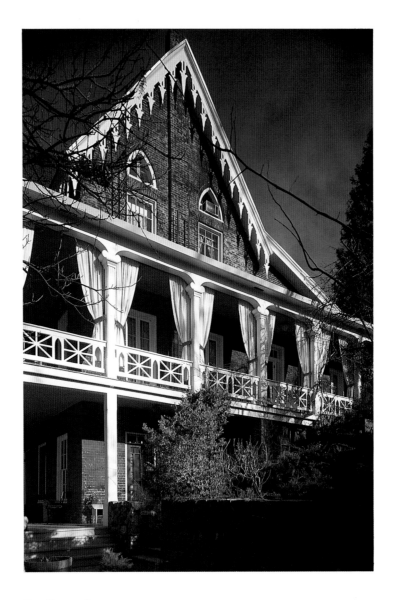

RED CASTLE INN

109 Prospect Street
Nevada City, CA 95959
Telephone: (916) 265-5135

Seven rooms and suites, each with private bath; one with woodburning
stove. Amenities include bathrobes and bubblebath. Candlelight breakfast
buffet with hot entree included; may be taken to your room. Saturday
night stays require two-night minimum, April through December and holidays. Smoking is not permitted. No handicapped access. Moderate.

Getting There
From Interstate 80 at Auburn, exit at Highway 49 and drive approximately
45 minutes to Nevada City. From Highway 49 in Nevada City, exit at
Sacramento Street; take first right on Adams; left on Prospect to inn.

RED CASTLE INN

Nevada City

*W*e romantics owe no small debt to those dedicated innkeepers who continue to rescue neglected, old mansions from certain demise, perform feats of restorative and decorative magic, and then invite us over to spend the night. Where would we go if places like Red Castle Inn had been allowed to fade away? Perish the thought.

It was in 1860 that self-proclaimed judge John Williams built his splendid Gothic revival mansion on Prospect Hill, visible throughout the town and from long distances. An architectural landmark, the mansion was christened The Red Castle by townsfolk who watched in awe as the stately, four-story brick building took shape.

A century later, the mansion abandoned and sagging, a farsighted admirer stepped in and bought the place. In 1963, a rejuvenated Red Castle (the Smithsonian Institution called it a perfect restoration) became one of California's first B&Bs.

Rooms for Romance

The mansion's builder wasn't simply showing off his wealth when he erected these multistories dripping with gothic ornamentation. With eleven children to shelter, building such a large house was a practical matter.

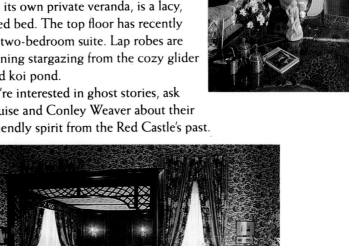

On the entry level is the Garden Room, which holds a canopied, queen-sized bed, French doors, and a small sitting area. One floor down (remember, the house sits against a hill), the Forest View Room, the most private in the house, is accessed via a private entrance. Inside this cozy hideaway, with its own private veranda, is a lacy, canopied, queen-sized bed. The top floor has recently been converted to a two-bedroom suite. Lap robes are available for late evening stargazing from the cozy glider near the fountain and koi pond.

By the way, if you're interested in ghost stories, ask innkeepers Mary Louise and Conley Weaver about their encounters with a friendly spirit from the Red Castle's past.

Hyatt Regency Lake Tahoe

Country Club Drive at Lakeshore
(P.O. Box 3239) Incline Village, NV 89450
Telephone: (702) 831-1111;
toll-free: (800) 233-1234

Four hundred sixty rooms, including twenty-four cottage units with fireplaces and decks. Restaurant,
lounge, casino. Smoking is allowed. Handicapped
access. Deluxe.

Getting There
From Interstate 80 at Truckee, take Highway 267 to
North Lake Tahoe. Turn left at Highway 28 to
Incline Village; right on Country Club Drive to hotel.

HYATT REGENCY LAKE TAHOE
Incline Village, NV

*W*hat's a chain hotel in Nevada doing in a romantic guide to California? OK, we cheated. Our visit happened to coincide with the reopening of the Hyatt, which emerged from a major facelift in 1990. A large part of the work involved demolishing and rebuilding the two-dozen lakeside cottages across the street from the hotel—to the tune of $4 million.

We've always considered Tahoe's north shore to be the lake's choicest spot, and the Hyatt's cottages are romantically situated to take full advantage of this prime location.

As a guest here, you won't have to fight crowds for a place to relax lakeside. The private beach—just outside your door—is reserved for guests only, and those staying in the cottages have direct access and gorgeous views. If you didn't come for the water, Hyatt's refurbished casino is just across the street.

Rooms for Romance

With river-rock trim, wood siding, and green roofs, the "old Tahoe"-styled cottage units were designed to blend in with their alpine surroundings. Also sharing the setting is a twenty-person, garden spa.

Rates for a one-bedroom cottage suite (including a sitting area, fireplace, king-sized bed, and kitchenette) are in the mid $400 range. The bedroom by itself (with two double beds, lake view, and deck or balcony, but no other special features) can be reserved for around $260 per night.

If you tell the reservations folks you're on your honeymoon, the Hyatt will set you up with a specially priced package that includes a one-bedroom cottage suite (fireplace, etc.), champagne, and breakfast in bed at nightly rates ranging from $400 to $500, depending on time of week and year.

Vizcaya

2019 Twenty First Street
Sacramento, CA 95818
Telephone: (916) 455-5243

Nine rooms, each with private bath; four with dual spa tubs and three with fireplaces. Full breakfast included. Smoking is not permitted. No handicapped access. Moderate to deluxe.

Getting There
Lettered streets intersect numbered streets in downtown Sacramento. The inn is near the corner of T and Twenty First streets.

VIZCAYA

Sacramento

Granted, the bedchambers in old-homes-turned-inns usually contain an inherently mystical intimacy that invites romance. But we've often found bed-and-breakfast bathrooms small, uninspired, and strictly functional. In some older inns, there aren't even enough bathrooms to go around.

At the other end of the spectrum, contemporary, upscale lodgings are increasingly beginning to focus much-needed attention on the bathroom as a special couples' retreat—but often at the expense of the bedroom.

Among the many hotels and inns along the path of our travels, we've uncovered few where bed and bath are combined in such near perfection as they are in, of all places, Sacramento. At Vizcaya, formerly known as the Driver Mansion Inn, and its sister establishment, the Sterling Hotel, bedrooms and bathrooms beckon with a come hither quality that makes a trip to the state capital worthwhile.

Rooms for Romance

Sandi Kann knew how to push our hot buttons when she and husband Richard, who runs the Sterling, created five particularly special baths to complement the comfortable Victorian decor at Vizcaya. In the main house, Room 4 boasts a bathroom equal in size to the bedroom. The marbled bath, which in fact originally was another bedroom, is situated in a corner and illuminated by leaded and stained glass. Underneath the windows sits a huge spa tub. There's also an oversized shower with glass walls. The adjoining bedroom holds a queen-sized bed with matching nightstands.

Equally appealing is the Carriage House, set at the rear of the property where a huge oak presides over a lawn and garden area with Victorian gazebo. Carriage House Three is a second-floor room decorated in blue and white with matching stained-glass; the room is furnished with wicker. The bed is king-sized and made of brass and iron. The bedroom is also equipped with a small woodburning stove.

The decadent bathroom has a sexy, black marble floor, pedestal sink, and skylight. There's an oversized, oval-shaped spa tub and, if you prefer to stand, a huge glass shower with double heads.

Carriage House Two, overlooking the courtyard, is styled in mauve tones and furnished with antiques, as well as a tiled fireplace. The bath features marble floors and wainscotting, pedestal sink, skylight, oval-shaped spa tub for two, and a spacious, double-head, glass and marble shower. The aforementioned three rooms are offered in the mid $150 range.

Because Sandi has recently built a grand reception center next to the inn, guests may encounter a wedding party or happy celebrants during a visit.

The Sterling Hotel

1300 H Street
Sacramento, CA 95814
Telephone: (916) 448-1300;
toll-free: (800) 365-7660

Twelve rooms, each with private bath and dual Jacuzzi tub.
Chanterelle is the Sterling's highly rated, greenhouse-style restaurant.
Smoking is not permitted. Handicapped access. Moderate to deluxe.

Getting There
Lettered streets intersect numbered streets in downtown Sacramento.
The hotel is at the intersection of Thirteenth and H streets.

STERLING HOTEL

Sacramento

When Richard Kann unveiled his grand plans to create a small, luxury hotel from a downtown Sacramento Victorian boardinghouse, more than a few scoffed. How fortunate for us that he persevered. And persevere he did, for when the dust had settled, not only had the skeptics eaten crow, even Kann's supporters were surprised.

The transformation, which required more than a little fairy dust, is extraordinary. While the Sterling incorporates most every contemporary comfort possible, the Victorian integrity of the building has been preserved. It's probably the finest small luxury hotel in inland Northern California.

With its convenient location, within three blocks of the state capitol, the Sterling is popular among visiting business types. However, it's also favored among visiting twosomes attracted by the romantic ambience and certain special touches. You see, this quaint establishment claims to be the only hotel in the nation to offer private, oversized Jacuzzis in each room.

Rooms for Romance

On the hotel's second floor, Room 202 (high $100 range on weekends) is often requested by couples. It faces the side of the property and is furnished with a beautiful wood-canopied, queen-sized bed that sits before a large window. The spacious bathroom has pink tile and stained-glass windows. Pedestal sinks and brass fixtures grace this and each of the other rooms. Each is also furnished with a large deck.

Room 304 is the bright, prominent corner bay room and one of the hotel's most popular. Next door in Room 303 (high $100 range on weekends), there's a balcony that overlooks magnolia trees in the front. This is a spacious room with Oriental carpet and one of the hotel's largest Jacuzzi tubs.

Room 302, set at the back of the building on the third floor (with a weekend rate in the low $100 range), is the smallest—and possibly the coziest—room in the house.

Ahwahnee Hotel

Yosemite Village
Yosemite National Park, CA 95389
Telephone: (209) 252-4848 for reservations

One hundred and twenty-three hotel and cottage
rooms. Swimming pool, restaurant, tennis court, and
lounge. Smoking is allowed in some rooms.
Handicapped access. Deluxe.

Getting There
The hotel is located in Yosemite Valley near the village. From Freeway 99 at Merced, follow Highway
140 (Yosemite exit) through Mariposa to the park.

AHWAHNEE HOTEL
Yosemite National Park

*I*f one were to list the man-made wonders of California, Yosemite's grand Ahwahnee Hotel would be assured a spot. Its location alone would place it near the top. This magnificent wood and stone fortress, dwarfed by the gleaming sheer granite cliffs of the Royal Arches, is probably the most dramatically situated (and popular) hotel in all of California.

Five thousand tons of stone were used in constructing this plush, six-story structure, which opened in 1927. Seven cottages containing twenty-two bedrooms were added the next year. Rates during those early days were $15 to $20 per night.

Although nightly tariffs are now in the low $200 range, the Ahwahnee continues to pack 'em in. Calling even one year in advance still might not ensure your chances of reserving a room during a peak period.

Set foot in this awe-inspiring hotel and you'll immediately see the attraction. A timeless American Indian theme (combined with some art deco flourishes) permeates the hotel, and the public spaces are spacious and inviting. Of particular note is the cavernous dining room with an open-raftered ceiling and peeled, sugar-pine log trusses. More than a dozen floor-to-ceiling windows afford spectacular views. We enjoyed a particularly romantic Valentine's Day dinner here while snow fell outside and sounds of a Steinway echoed through the hall.

Rooms for Romance

Because of the extraordinarily high occupancy rate here, it's difficult—but not impossible—

to reserve a specific room. The rooms where President Kennedy (the Presidential Suite) and Queen Elizabeth (the Queen's Suite) stayed with their spouses are most coveted. Two of the bedrooms comprising the Presidential Suite have access to a balcony affording a 180-degree vista from El Capitan to Half Dome. Rooms 232 and 234 have their own balconies.

For a more woodsy experience, many guests prefer the Ahwahnee's upscale cottages, which offer a charm unique in the valley. Because the cottages have no air conditioning and because they are a slushy stroll away from the main hotel building in the winter, we recommend these units only for fall and spring getaways.

One of the Ahwahnee's prime attractions is the annual Bracebridge Dinner, a Renaissance Christmas feast and musical celebration. So popular is this event that you will have to win a lottery to attend. It's a long shot, at best, as some 60,000 annually compete for the opportunity to break bread with Squire Bracebridge in medieval splendor.

WAWONA HOTEL

Wawona

Yosemite National Park, CA 95389

Telephone: (209) 252-4848 for reservations

One hundred and five rooms, fifty of which have private baths. Swimming pool, golf course, tennis court, and restaurant. Smoking is not permitted in Clark Cottage and the main building. Handicapped access. Moderate.

Getting There

From Fresno (eighty miles), take Highway 41 north. From Mariposa, take 49 east to Oakhurst, then north on Highway 41.

WAWONA HOTEL

Yosemite National Park

Situated at the southern edge of one America's most visited national parks, the village of Wawona might best be described as "the other Yosemite." Although the area has served travelers for hundreds of years (the Indians called it Pallachun, which meant "a good place to stop"), it's remarkably quiet here, compared to the bustling valley, with its tour buses, shops, and camping grounds.

True, you won't find quite the dramatic grandeur of Half Dome and El Capitan. But Wawona offers Yosemite visitors a rare chance to savor the park's unspoiled beauty—without donning a backpack and hitting the trail.

The Wawona Hotel has been a favorite destination of savvy Yosemite visitors since the mid-1850s, when a rustic guesthouse was erected. When the automobile made Yosemite more accessible, the owners responded with more accommodations. Today, several vintage buildings comprise the Wawona Hotel compound.

The ensuing years may have brought upgrades in creature comforts, but visitors will see plenty of evidence of the early days, such as graceful verandas, clawfoot tubs, steam radiators, and brass doorknobs. An old, hand-crank phone still connects the Victorian-style Annex to the main desk.

Rooms for Romance

The most prized rooms at the Wawona Hotel are found in Little White, a picture perfect Victorian cottage with all the trimmings. Inside is updated, Laura Ashley-style decor. (One of the cottage's three rooms has a private bath.)

We also enjoyed a stay in the vintage Annex. Our room, 137, was one of the hotel's largest and featured a clawfoot tub. Outside, a wide covered porch invited lazy lounging. Picturesque Clark Cottage houses another set of nice rooms.

The hotel is open daily from around Easter through Thanksgiving, and on weekends only during the winter. At the time of our last visit, rooms carried rates ranging from around $65 to around $90.

Appendix

More Travel Resources for Incurable Romantics

Weekends for Two in Northern California, Volume II: 50 More Romantic Getaways (1995)
Weekends for Two in Southern California: 50 Romantic Getaways
Weekends for Two in the Pacific Northwest: 50 Romantic Getaways

Each with more than 150 color photos, these are the definitive travel guides to the West's most romantic destinations.

By Bill Gleeson
Chronicle Books

Index

Our Travel Journal

Getaway date:

Getaway destination:

Our room name/number:

Memories we made: